Collins

Revision

NEW GCSE SCIENCE

Biology

for AQA A Higher

Authors: Gemma Young and Sarah Jinks

Revision guide +
Exam practice workbook

William Collins' dream of knowledge for all began with the publication of his first book in 1819. A self-educated mill worker, he not only enriched millions of lives, but also founded a flourishing publishing house. Today, staying true to this spirit, Collins books are packed with inspiration, innovation and practical expertise. They place you at the centre of a world of possibility and give you exactly what you need to explore it.

Collins. Freedom to teach

Published by Collins
An imprint of HarperCollinsPublishers
77–85 Fulham Palace Road
Hammersmith
London
W6 8JB

Browse the complete Collins catalogue at
www.collinseducation.com

ISBN 978-0-00-741606-6

British Library Cataloguing in Publication Data
A Catalogue record for this publication is available from the British Library.

Project managed by Hart McLeod Limited, Cambridge.

Edited, proofread, indexed and designed by
Hart McLeod Limited, Cambridge.

Printed and bound in China

Acknowledgements
The Authors and Publishers are grateful to the following for permission to reproduce photographs.

p8 ©Hank Morgan/Science Photo Library; p15 ©Roman Kobzarev/istock.com; p24 & p55 ©Michael Eichelberger, Visuals Unlimited/Science Photo Library; p79 left ©Gabor Izso/istock.com, p79 right ©Klemiantsou Kanstantsin/istock.com; p84 ©Karl Dolenc/istock.com

About this book

This book covers the content you will need to revise for GCSE Biology AQA A Higher. It is designed to help you get the best grade in your GCSE Biology Higher Exam.

The content exactly matches the topics you will be studying for your examinations. The book is divided into two major parts: **Revision guide** and **Workbook**.

Begin by revising a topic in the Revision guide section, then test yourself by answering the exam-style questions for that topic in the Workbook section.

Workbook answers are provided in a detachable section at the end of the book.

Revision guide

The Revision guide (pages 6–52) summarises the content of the exam specification and acts as a memory jogger. The material is divided into grades. There is a question (**Improve your grade**) on each page that will help you to check your progress. Typical answers to these questions and examiner's comments, are provided at the end of the Revision guide section (pages 53–58) for you to compare with your responses. This will help you to improve your answers in the future.

At the end of each module, you will find a **Summary** page. This highlights some important facts from each module.

Workbook

The Workbook (pages 67–116) allows you to work at your own pace on some typical exam-style questions. You will find that the actual GCSE questions are more likely to test knowledge and understanding across topics. However, the aim of the Revision guide and Workbook is to guide you through each topic so that you can identify your areas of strength and weakness.

The Workbook also contains example questions that require longer answers (**Extended response questions**). You will find one question that is similar to these in each section of your written exam papers. The quality of your written communication will be assessed when you answer these questions in the exam, so practise writing longer answers, using sentences. The **Answers** to all the questions in the Workbook are detachable for flexible practice and can be found on pages 121–131.

At the end of the Workbook there is a series of **Revision checklists** that you can use to tick off the topics when you are confident about them and understand certain key ideas.

Additional features

Throughout the Revision Guide there are **Exam tips** to give additional exam advice, **Remember boxes** pick out key facts and a series of **How Science Works** features, all to aid your revision.

The **Glossary** allows quick reference to the definitions of scientific terms covered in the Revision guide.

Contents

B3 Biology

Diet and energy

Diet and metabolic rate

D–C

- People should eat a **balanced diet** which contains some of all these different kinds of nutrients:
  - carbohydrates, fats and protein for energy
  - small amounts of vitamins and mineral ions for keeping healthy.

- If your diet is not balanced, you may become **malnourished** (become too fat or too thin, or suffer from deficiency diseases).

- To lose body mass, people may go on a **slimming diet** where they eat less. Exercising more also helps. These both lead to more energy being used up than is taken in, and the body is forced to use up some of its stored fat for energy.

- **Metabolic rate** is the rate at which chemical reactions take place in your cells.

- The greater the proportion of muscle to fat in the body, the higher the metabolic rate is likely to be. It also increases during exercise.

- Metabolic rate can be affected by your genes, which you inherit from your parents.

> **Remember!**
> A balanced diet will contain all nutrients in the correct amounts.

How Science Works

- Some slimming programmes and products may make claims that are unrealistic. Also it is important to remember that people will put back on the mass they lost if they don't change their eating habits for good.

Fatty foods

B–A*

- One gram of fat releases almost twice as much energy as one gram of carbohydrate, or one gram of protein.

- Proteins are not usually a major source of energy for the body because they are used for the more important functions of growth and repair.

Diet, exercise and health

Diet and cholesterol

D–C

- A high level of **cholesterol** in the blood increases the risk of developing plaques in the walls of the arteries. Figure 1 shows how this can happen.

- Sometimes, a clot blocks one of the arteries that take oxygenated blood to the heart muscle. This causes a heart attack – the muscle cannot work, so the heart cannot beat properly.

- Eating saturated fats (those found in animal products) raises blood cholesterol levels. Unsaturated fats, found in plants, seem to lower blood cholesterol level.

- Some people's bodies are better than others at keeping low levels of cholesterol in their blood. They have inherited this from their parents.

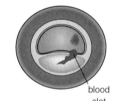

A healthy artery has a stretchy wall and a space in the middle for blood to pass through.

Sometimes, a substance called plaque builds up in the wall. This is more likely to happen if you have a lot of cholesterol in your blood.

The plaque slows down the blood and a clot may form. A part of the plaque may break away.

Figure 1: How a plaque develops in an artery

Good and bad cholesterol

B–A*

- Cholesterol is carried in your blood in two ways, as:
  - low-density lipoprotein (LDL) cholesterol, which is 'bad' and can cause heart disease
  - high-density lipoprotein (HDL) cholesterol, which is 'good' as it can protect against heart disease by helping to remove cholesterol from the walls of blood vessels.

Improve your grade

Harry's diet is very high in saturated fats. Suggest two ways that this could affect his health. **AO2 (3 marks)**

Pathogens and infections

Disease

- Microorganisms that cause disease are called pathogens.
- Bacteria can reproduce rapidly inside the body. They may produce toxins (poisons) that make us feel ill.
- Viruses reproduce inside a body cell then destroy it when they burst out. The viruses then invade other cells.
- An epidemic occurs when a wide spread of people have a disease. A pandemic is when the disease affects a whole country or goes worldwide.
- In the 1840s, a doctor called Semmelweis used evidence from the death rates of women to work out that they were dying because doctors were transferring something to them from dead bodies. He made all the doctors wash their hands in chlorine water and, within a very short time, the death rate plummeted. We now know the infection that killed the women was caused by bacteria.

A new hypothesis

- Scientists are still learning about pathogens.

How Science Works

- Doctors once thought that stomach ulcers were caused by stress or over-secretion of acid in the stomach. In 1982, two Australian researchers, Marshall and Warren, found bacteria in the stomachs of people with ulcers. Their hypothesis was that these bacteria caused the ulcers. The evidence to prove it came when Warren swallowed some of the bacteria and developed a stomach ulcer.

Fighting infection

Phagocytosis and lymphocytes

- Figure 2 shows how a type of white blood cell, called a phagocyte, can surround and ingest bacteria. This activity is called phagocytosis.

- Lymphocytes produce chemicals called antibodies. The antibodies group round and stick to the pathogen. This may kill it directly, or stick it to other pathogens in clumps so that the phagocytes can destroy them more easily.

1 A phagocyte moves towards a bacterium   2 The phagocyte pushes a sleeve of cytoplasm outwards to surround the bacterium   3 The bacterium is now enclosed in a vacuole inside the cell. It is then killed and digested by enzymes

Figure 2: Phagocytosis

- Some lymphocytes make antitoxins that can stick to the toxins given off by bacteria, and destroy them.

- Both antibodies and antitoxins are very specific – each kind only works against a particular pathogen or toxin.

More about antibodies

- This is an antibody molecule. The bits on the end of the Y arms can come in millions of different shapes. Each lymphocyte can make just one kind. The end bits fit onto molecules on the pathogen. Each shape only fits onto one kind of pathogen.

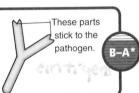

Figure 3: A simplified antibody molecule

These parts stick to the pathogen.

Improve your grade

Use the graph on the right to explain the change in the number of pathogens. **AO2 (4 marks)**

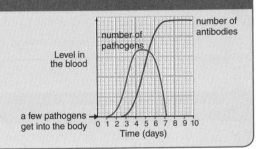

number of antibodies

number of pathogens

Level in the blood

a few pathogens get into the body

Time (days)

Drugs against disease

Antibiotics

- Antibiotics are drugs that kill bacteria inside your body, without killing your own cells. Examples are penicillin and streptomycin.
- Antibiotics do not all work equally well against all the kinds of bacteria.
- Figure 1 shows how we find the best antibiotic to kill a bacterium. Bacteria are spread onto a jelly. Paper discs soaked in different antibiotics are placed on the jelly and the antibiotics diffuse out. If the antibiotic kills the bacteria, they do not grow around the disc.

> **Remember!**
> Antibiotics cannot destroy viruses. Some viral infections can be treated by taking antiviral drugs.

EXAM TIP
You may be shown an image of a test like this and be asked what it shows. The clear jelly shows no bacterial growth: so the bigger this area, the more effective the antibiotic. In this case, antibiotic E is the most effective.

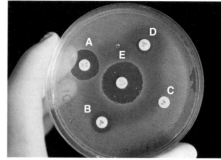

Figure 1: Testing antibiotics

Prescribing antibiotics

- Scientists now know that people must not use antibiotics unnecessarily. Overuse makes it more likely that bacteria will become resistant to them.

Antibiotic resistance

Reducing the risk

- Bacteria do not become resistant to antibiotics on purpose. It happens by natural selection. Figure 2 shows how.

- As new antibiotic-resistant strains of bacteria emerge, we have to find new antibiotics to kill them.

This is a population of bacteria in someone's body. By chance, one of them has mutated and is slightly different from the others.

The person takes antibiotics to kill the bacteria. It works – except on the single odd bacterium. This one is resistant to the antibiotic.

The bacterium now has no competitors and grows rapidly. It divides and makes lots of identical copies of itself. There is now a population of bacteria that the antibiotic cannot kill. This process is an example of **natural selection**.

Figure 2: How antibiotic resistance arises

- To reduce the chance of new strains forming, we need to reduce the use of antibiotics.

- Whenever antibiotics are used, it gives an advantage to any mutant bacterium that happens to be resistant to them.

- If they are not used, then a mutant bacterium does not have any advantage: it is no more likely to reproduce than any other bacterium.

MRSA deaths

- MRSA (methicillin-resistant *Staphylococcus aureus*) is sometimes called a superbug because it is resistant to most antibiotics.
- The number of deaths from MRSA rose between 1993 and 2006, but it is now gradually decreasing as people become more aware of how to stop it spreading.

Improve your grade

Explain why a doctor will not prescribe you antibiotics for a bacterial throat infection. **AO2 (3 marks)**

Vaccination

MMR

- In the UK, children have the MMR vaccination which makes them immune to measles, mumps and rubella.

- A small amount of the dead or inactive viruses that cause the diseases are injected into the blood.

- The white blood cells attack them, just as they would attack living pathogens. They remember how to make the antibody, so the child is now immune to the diseases without having to suffer them first.

How Science Works

- In 1998, a group of scientists published an article suggesting that the MMR vaccination might cause autism. Many parents decided not to let their child have the MMR vaccination, even though there was no evidence in the article. Many studies have been carried out since. No one has found any link between the MMR vaccination and autism.

New diseases

- New infectious diseases appear when mutations occur in bacteria or viruses.

- For example in 2009, a new kind of flu virus, called swine flu, spread quickly to all parts of the world. As existing flu vaccines would not work against it, new ones had to be developed.

Remember!
Some diseases cannot be vaccinated against because there are too many strains of the pathogen. An example of this is the common cold, which is caused by over 250 different types of virus.

Growing bacteria

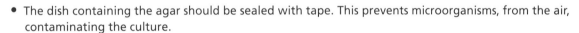

Avoiding contamination

- The microorganisms growing on the nutrient medium are called a culture.

- You should use a sterile technique to stop unwanted microorganisms from entering the nutrient medium.

- All equipment, including the medium, should be sterilised before use.

- Metal equipment, such as a wire inoculating loop, can be held in a flame.

- You must not touch the nutrient jelly (agar) with your fingers or breathe over it.

- The dish containing the agar should be sealed with tape. This prevents microorganisms, from the air, contaminating the culture.

- You should keep the cultures lower than 25 °C. If you keep them warmer then this might encourage the growth of microorganisms that live in the body, which are more likely to be pathogens.

Pathology and industrial laboratories

- Bacteria that are causing an illness in a patient may be grown in a hospital pathology lab.

- The Petri dishes, on which the bacteria are growing, will be put into an incubator to keep them warm and to encourage rapid growth.

- In industrial labs, harmless bacteria are grown commercially, for example, to make enzymes.

Improve your grade

You wish to grow some harmless *E. coli* bacteria on some agar jelly. You use an inoculating loop to transfer the bacteria to the jelly. Explain why it is important to hold the inoculating loop in a flame first. **AO1 (2 marks)**

Co-ordination, nerves and hormones

Nerves and hormones

D–C

- Nerves contain special cells called nerve cells, which transmit impulses to and from the brain and spinal cord (the central nervous system).
- Glands secrete chemicals called hormones into the blood. The bloodstream carries the hormones around the body.
- Most hormones affect just a few different organs. These are called their target organs.
- An example of a hormone is adrenaline, which affects the heart, breathing muscles, eyes and digestive system.

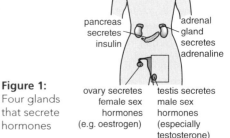

Figure 1: Four glands that secrete hormones

pancreas secretes insulin

adrenal gland secretes adrenaline

ovary secretes female sex hormones (e.g. oestrogen)

testis secretes male sex hormones (especially testosterone)

Response duration

B–A*

- A nervous response, for example touching a football, is fast and short-lived because impulses travelling along nerves only take a short time.

- Where a longer-term response is needed, hormones are often a more appropriate method of communication.

Receptors

Neurones

D–C

- Information is carried in the nervous system as electrical impulses. The cells that transmit these impulses are called nerve cells or neurones.

- The neurones that transmit impulses from receptors to the central nervous system are called sensory neurones.

- The neurones that transmit impulses from the central nervous system to effectors are called motor neurones.

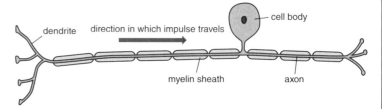

dendrite · direction in which impulse travels · cell body · myelin sheath · axon

Figure 2: A sensory neurone

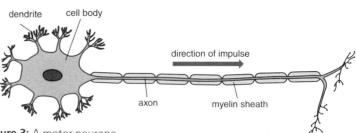

dendrite · cell body · direction of impulse · axon · myelin sheath

Figure 3: A motor neurone

Remember!
Receptors detect stimuli and send an impulse along a neurone. Effectors (muscles and glands) respond to the stimuli.

EXAM TIP
Make sure you use the correct science words in your answers. Use 'impulses' rather than 'messages'; and 'neurone' if you are talking about a single cell or 'nerve' if you are talking about a bundle of them, as in the spinal cord.

Rod cells

B–A*

- Rod cells at the back of the eye (retina) are sensitive to light.
- If only one photon of light falls onto a rod cell, this is enough to make it generate an electrical impulse which is sent along the optic nerve to the brain.
- The brain uses the pattern of impulses, arriving from different parts of the retina, to construct a 'picture' of the world you are looking at.

Improve your grade

An injury that results in breaking of the spine may result in the person being paralysed. Explain why. **AO2 (3 marks)**

Reflex actions

Impulse pathways

- A reflex arc is the pathway taken by a nerve impulse as it passes from a receptor, through the central nervous system, and finally to an effector.

- Figure 4 shows the path the impulses take.

- It takes a nerve impulse only a fraction of a second to go along this route. That is why reflex actions are so quick.

- The gaps between neurones are called synapses.

- Electrical impulses cannot jump across synapses. When an impulse gets to the end of a neurone, it causes a chemical to be secreted. The chemical diffuses across the gap and starts an electrical impulse along the next neurone.

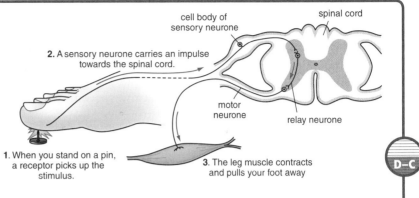

2. A sensory neurone carries an impulse towards the spinal cord.

cell body of sensory neurone

spinal cord

motor neurone

relay neurone

1. When you stand on a pin, a receptor picks up the stimulus.

3. The leg muscle contracts and pulls your foot away

Figure 4: A reflex arc

Remember! Synapses slow down the speed of the impulse.

D–C

Conscious control

- Synapses enable us to respond to a stimulus in more than one way. For example, the relay neurone, in the spinal cord, will have synapses to other neurones that can carry nerve impulses down from the brain.

- This allows us to take conscious control of our response to a stimulus.

B–A*

Controlling the body

Temperature control

- You gain water from food and drink. You lose water in your breath, sweat and urine.

- Your blood has ions dissolved in it, such as those found in salt.

- The kidneys help to keep the balance of water and ions by varying the amount of water and salt excreted from your body in urine.

- Human body temperature needs to be kept at around 37 °C, as this is the temperature at which our enzymes work best.

- The body loses heat by radiation from the skin, and from the evaporation of sweat.

- The body also has mechanisms to keep the concentration of sugar in the blood constant.

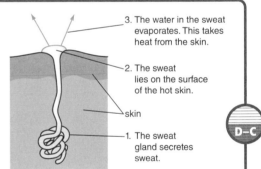

3. The water in the sweat evaporates. This takes heat from the skin.

2. The sweat lies on the surface of the hot skin.

skin

1. The sweat gland secretes sweat.

Figure 5: How sweating helps you to lose heat

D–C

Survival in the desert

- An SAS survival manual gives this advice to conserve water: avoid exertion, keep cool and stay in the shade; don't lie on the hot ground; don't eat, because digestion uses up fluids; talk as little as possible; and breathe through your nose rather than your mouth.

B–A*

Improve your grade

James is dancing in a nightclub. He starts to sweat. Explain how sweating helps to cool him down. **AO2 (2 marks)**

Reproductive hormones

Hormones and the menstrual cycle

- At the start of the menstrual cycle, the pituitary gland secretes FSH (follicle-stimulating hormone). This causes an **egg to mature** in one of the woman's ovaries and also stimulates the **ovary to secrete oestrogen**.
- **Oestrog**en makes the **inner lining of the uterus grow thicker.** High levels of oestrogen stop the **production of FSH.**
- Luteinising hormone (LH) stimulates the **release of eggs** from the ovary.
- As the level of FSH drops, the ovary stops secreting oestrogen. This cuts off the inhibition of FSH secretion, so the cycle starts all over again.
- The **contraceptive pill** may contain oestrogen. It stops FSH being produced, so that eggs do not mature.

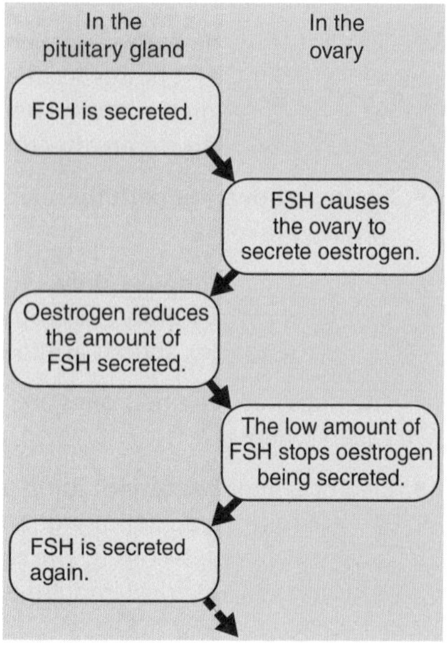

How Science Works

- When the pill was first used it produced many **side effects,** for example people put on weight. Nowadays, the pills contain much **less oestrogen** than they used to (some have no oestrogen at all but contain another hormone called **progesterone**), so there are fewer side effects.

In the pituitary gland	In the ovary
FSH is secreted.	
	FSH causes the ovary to secrete oestrogen.
Oestrogen reduces the amount of FSH secreted.	
	The low amount of FSH stops oestrogen being secreted.
FSH is secreted again.	

Figure 1: FSH and oestrogen secretion

> ### Remember!
> FSH and LH are produced in the pituitary gland which is in the brain. They reach their target organs (the uterus and the ovary) through the bloodstream.

Co-ordinating the menstrual cycle

- The change in **concentration** of oestrogen causes changes in the **thickness of the uterus lining.** The rise in oestrogen concentration causes the uterus lining to thicken. When oestrogen concentration falls below a certain point, the uterus lining breaks down.
- The release of an egg from the ovary usually happens at about day 14 of the cycle. It is called ovulation.

Controlling fertility

IVF

- IVF stands for 'in vitro fertilisation'.
- The woman is given hormones, such as FSH, to make her ovaries produce several eggs.
- The eggs are removed and are mixed with her partner's sperm for fertilisation to occur.
- One of the embryos is chosen and placed in the woman's uterus. With luck, it will sink into the uterus lining and develop as a fetus.

Multiple births

- Twins or triplets are more likely to have problems developing in the uterus than a single fetus. They are also more likely to be underweight at birth.

> ### EXAM TIP
> Multiple births are more common with women who have used fertility treatments. You should be able to explain why this is.

Improve your grade

FSH is found in fertility drugs. Explain how taking FSH will increase a woman's fertility. **AO2 (2 marks)**

Plant responses and hormones

Phototropism and gravitropism

- A growth response to light is a tropism called phototropism.

- Auxin is a plant hormone which makes cells in shoots get longer. When light shines onto a shoot, the auxin builds up on the shady side. This makes the cells on that side get longer. So, the shoot bends towards the light.

- A growth response to gravity is called gravitropism or geotropism.

- Auxin tends to accumulate on the lower side of a root. In roots, auxin reduces the rate of growth. So, the lower side of the shoot grows more slowly than the upper surface. This causes the root to bend downwards.

- Gardeners dip the base of a cutting into a powder or gel called rooting hormone, which makes the cutting grow roots.

- Plant hormones are also used as weedkillers. The hormones make the weeds grow very fast and then die. The hormones only affect weeds because they have a different metabolism.

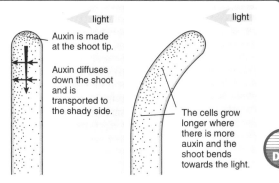

light   light

Auxin is made at the shoot tip.

Auxin diffuses down the shoot and is transported to the shady side.

The cells grow longer where there is more auxin and the shoot bends towards the light.

Figure 2: How auxin makes a shoot grow towards the light

D–C

Where are the receptors in a plant?

- Scientists in the past carried out experiments to work out how plants detect stimuli.

How Science Works

- This experiment shows that it is the tip of the shoot that detects light.

Method

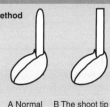

A Normal

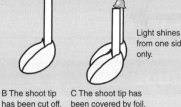

B The shoot tip has been cut off.

C The shoot tip has been covered by foil.

Light shines from one side only.

Results

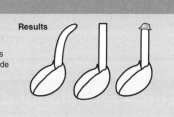

B–A*

Drugs

Dangers of drugs

- Some people take drugs because they make them feel different. This is called recreational drug use.

- Many recreational drugs are legal but still can be harmful, such as alcohol.

- Some recreational drugs are illegal because of the harm they can cause. Cannabis is an example, it may cause mental illness.

- A drug addiction can have dangerous long-term effects. Over time, the lungs, brain and liver can be seriously damaged.

- If someone is addicted to a drug, they may suffer from very unpleasant withdrawal symptoms if they stop taking it.

D–C

Deaths from drug use

- Each year, thousands of people in Britain die from misusing drugs.

- Some deaths are from poisoning. Some happen because drugs can affect the brain, making people behave in a dangerous way.

B–A*

Improve your grade

Explain how the hormone auxin brings about a response to light called phototropism. **AO2 (4 marks)**

Developing new drugs

Drug trials

- A drug trial, on a potential new medicine, contains three stages.

  1 The drug is tested in a laboratory on human cells or tissues to find out if it is toxic (poisonous). It may be also be tested on live animals.
  2 Human volunteers are given different doses, to find out what is the highest dose that can be taken safely. Any side-effects are recorded.
  3 In clinical trials, the drug is tested on its target illness. It is given to people who have the illness, to see if it makes them better. Some patients are given placebos which do not contain the drug. Neither the patient nor their doctor knows whether they have a placebo or the real drug (a double-blind trial). This helps determine whether the drug really works.

How Science Works

- In the 1960s, many pregnant women were prescribed the drug thalidomide to treat 'morning sickness' in pregnancy.
  The drug had been thoroughly trialled as a sleeping pill, but no one had thought to test it on pregnant women. Women who took thalidomide in early pregnancy often gave birth to babies with short arms or no arms.
  Thalidomide was banned worldwide, but it is now being used to treat serious diseases such as leprosy.

Evaluating statins

- Statins are drugs that help people to reduce their blood cholesterol level and therefore greatly reduce their risk of getting heart disease.

- When statins were first introduced, trials had shown almost no side-effects.

- However, since then, side-effects such as painful muscles have been discovered.

Legal and illegal drugs

Dangers from recreational drugs

- Alcohol and nicotine cause far more illness and death each year than all the illegal drugs put together.

- People do not worry so much about them because they have been around for so long, and because so many people use them.

Drugs in sport

- Professional sports people are banned from taking certain performance-enhancing drugs because they could give them an unfair advantage. For example:
  - steroids can stimulate the body to grow larger, stronger muscles
  - beta blockers can help someone to stay calm and steady
  - stimulants can increase the heart rate.

- These drugs can often cause long-lasting damage or even death.

Improve your grade

Some doctors believe that everyone over the age of 50 should be prescribed statins on the NHS for free. Evaluate this decision. AO2 (4 marks)

Competition

Competing

- Organisms may have to compete for resources if they are in short supply.

- For example, plants compete for light – the ones that grow tallest win the competition.

- The individuals best at competing are the most likely to survive. Those not good at getting resources are the most likely to die.

- If there are not enough females to go around, then males will compete for a mate.

- Animals may also compete for a territory – a space in which they can find food and a place to breed.

Remember!
Competition does not usually mean that organisms actually fight over resources. They just have to find ways of being better at getting them than others are.

Figure 1: Stags fight over the right to mate with the females in the herd

Avoiding competition

- Many organisms have become able to live in places where few others can survive. Although these places make survival tough, there is no need to share resources.

- This can increase chances of surviving and having large numbers of offspring.

Adaptations for survival

Living in difficult climates

- Plants that live in **dry places** usually have:
  - long, wide-spreading roots – the roots grow **deep** into the soil, to **reach** water
  - small or no leaves – the smaller the leaf surface area, the less the amount of **water** evaporating away
  - tissues that can **store** water.

Remember!
Plants and animals must have features that allow them to survive in their habitat. These features are adaptations.

- Animals that live in dry places must be able to manage without much water. For example, camels' **stomachs** can hold over **20 litres** of water, they can drink very quickly, **store** water as fat in their humps, and they produce very little urine.

- Desert animals often have **large ears**. A large surface area helps the animal lose body heat and stay cool.

- Animals that live in very cold places, such as the Arctic, often have **thick fur and thick layers of fat**. This insulation helps the animal **reduce heat loss**. They are coloured white, for camouflage against snow.

- Many plants and animals have thorns, poisons and warning colours to deter predators.

Extreme environments

- Organisms that can live in very difficult environments are called extremophiles. They are usually **microorganisms**.

- For most organisms, conditions such as high temperatures and high pressure would be lethal.

- Extremophiles must have very stable protein molecules that are not affected by these conditions.

EXAM TIP

Make sure you can describe how the camel and one animal from the Arctic, for example a polar bear, are adapted.

Improve your grade

Explain how cacti are adapted to living in the dry desert. **AO2 (3 marks)**

Environmental change

Causes of change

- Environmental changes are caused by living and non-living factors. For example:
  - non-living factors include global warming, which has caused rainfall in central Australia to decrease
  - living factors include the introduction of the grey squirrel into Britain, which caused a decrease in the population of the native red squirrel.

The disappearing bees

- Honeybees help pollinate flowers that will develop into food crops.
- In recent years, there has been a decline in the numbers of honeybees.
- We are not sure of the cause but various suggestions have been put forward to explain it.

Pollution indicators

Measuring changes in the environment

- In the UK, the composition of the air and of the water in rivers and streams; and the air temperature and rainfall, are constantly being measured. This makes sure that any changes can be tracked.

- Oxygen meters measure the concentration of dissolved oxygen in the water. Unpolluted water contains a lot of dissolved oxygen.

- Thermometers measure temperature. Rain gauges measure rainfall.

- Scientists can use the distribution of living organisms to find out about pollution. For example:
  - if there is a lot of sulfur dioxide in the air, many species of lichens will not be able to grow
  - if there is not very much oxygen in a river, there will be no oxygen-loving mayfly larvae in the water, instead there will be just rat-tailed maggots and bloodworms.

Remember!
The higher the number of different lichen species that can grow in an area, the lower the levels of sulfur dioxide in the air.

Sewage pollution and invertebrates

- Polluted water often contains very little dissolved oxygen. Some species of invertebrate are able to live in this water, but others are not. Figure 1 shows some of these species.

EXAM TIP

You do not have to memorise this diagram but you may be asked to apply the information it contains.

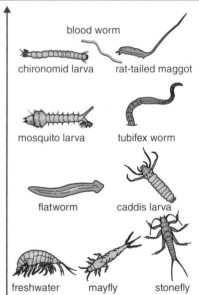

Figure 1: Invertebrates that can be used as pollution indicators

Improve your grade

Sewage contains a lot of microorganisms. Explain why mayfly larva cannot live in water polluted with sewage.
AO2 (2 marks)

Food chains and energy flow

Energy wastage

- Green plants capture only a small amount of energy from the light that falls onto them. This is because some light:
  - misses the leaves altogether
  - hits the leaf and reflects back from the leaf surface
  - hits the leaf, but goes all the way through without hitting any chlorophyll
  - hits the chlorophyll, but is not absorbed because it is of the wrong wavelength (colour).

- As a result, very little of the light energy that falls on a plant can be used for photosynthesis and get transferred into chemical energy in carbohydrates and other substances.

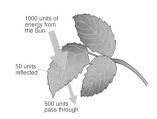

Figure 2: This is what happens to energy from the Sun that falls onto a leaf

 D–C

Remember!

A food chain shows that energy is passed from producer (plants) to consumers. Consumers gain their energy by eating the organism before it in the food chain.

Efficiency

- Whenever energy is transferred, some of it is wasted.

- To calculate the efficiency of energy transfer, use the formula:

$$\text{efficiency} = \frac{\text{useful energy transferred} \times 100\%}{\text{original amount of energy}}$$

EXAM TIP

If you are asked to calculate efficiency, you will be supplied with this formula. However, you should practice using it in preparation for the exam.

B–A*

Biomass

Energy losses

- Figure 3 shows a pyramid of biomass drawn to scale. Its shape is explained by the fact that whenever energy is transferred, some is wasted (not used for useful work). So at each step, there is less energy available for the organisms to use. Less energy means less biomass.

- The food chain loses energy because:
  - some materials and energy are lost in the waste materials produced by each organism, such as carbon dioxide, urine and faeces
  - respiration in each organism's cells releases energy from nutrients to be used for movement and other purposes, so much of this energy is eventually lost as heat to the surroundings
  - not all of the organism's tissues are eaten, for example the antelope does not eat the roots of the grass as they are under the ground.

Figure 3: A pyramid of biomass drawn to scale

mass of lion

mass of antelope

mass of grass

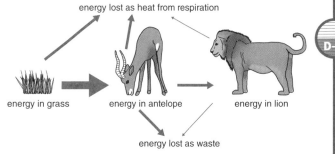

energy lost as heat from respiration

energy in grass

energy in antelope

energy in lion

energy lost as waste

Figure 4: How energy is wasted as it passes along a food chain

 D–C

More about energy loss

- Mammals and birds use glucose to provide energy to keep their body temperature high.

- This means that energy loss from birds and mammals is high.

- Other animals, such as snakes, frogs and fish, just stay the same temperature as their environment.

 B–A*

Improve your grade

Explain why biomass decreases as you move along a food chain. **AO2 (3 marks)**

Decay

Speeding or slowing decay

- Most of the bacteria and fungi that carry out decay need:
  - oxygen for aerobic respiration
  - a warm temperature for their enzymes to work at an optimum rate
  - moisture for reproduction.

- Increasing the temperature of microorganisms slows or stops decay.

Remember!

Compost heaps are kept warm, moist and aerated to speed up the decay of plant waste into compost. Compost is high in nutrients and is used to promote plant growth.

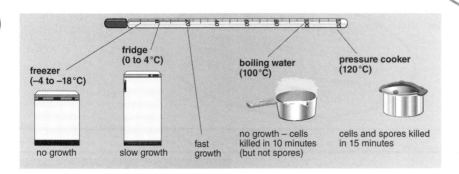

freezer (−4 to −18°C)

fridge (0 to 4°C)

boiling water (100°C)

pressure cooker (120°C)

no growth

slow growth

fast growth

no growth – cells killed in 10 minutes (but not spores)

cells and spores killed in 15 minutes

Figure 1: How temperature affects the activity of microorganisms

Preventing decay

- If food is not to decay, it can be treated so as to slow down or stop the activity of microorganisms.

- Examples of this include canning, pickling and drying food.

EXAM TIP

You should be able to apply your knowledge to explain how these methods of food preservation help to slow down decay.

Recycling

Recycling and food chains

- Figure 2 shows how microorganisms fit into a simple food chain.

- You can see that these decay microorganisms feed on every organism in the chain.

- They will break down most of the waste material that the plants and animals produce, and then their bodies will be broken down by others when they die.

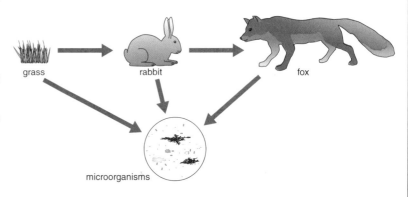

grass

rabbit

fox

microorganisms

Figure 2: A food chain, including the decay organisms

Dead whales

- Whole communities of organisms use whale carcasses as food.
- Crabs, worms and fish eat the whale's body.
- Microorganisms gradually decay the whale's tissues. The whole process can take decades.

Improve your grade

Write a simple plan for an investigation to prove that the decay of bread by mould requires moisture.
AO2 (2 marks)

The carbon cycle

Processes in the carbon cycle

- Animals, plants and decomposers all interact with each other in the carbon cycle (Figure 3).

- Photosynthesis converts carbon dioxide into carbohydrates and other food molecules such as proteins:
carbon dioxide + water → glucose + oxygen

- When animals eat plants (or another animal) the food goes into their cells and is broken down by respiration: glucose + oxygen → carbon dioxide + water

- Carbon dioxide is returned to the air when the animal breathes out.

- Plants and microorganisms also respire.

- Some dead organisms do not decay. They become buried and compressed, deep underground and change into fossil fuels.

- Carbon dioxide is returned to the air when wood or fossil fuels are burnt (combustion).

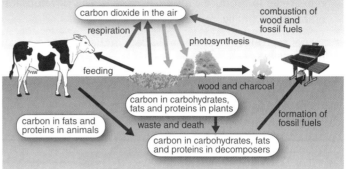

Figure 3: How carbon is recycled in the carbon cycle

Energy in the carbon cycle

- Energy is transferred in the carbon cycle.

- During photosynthesis, energy from sunlight is transferred to energy stores as chemicals in carbohydrates.

- Some of this energy is transferred to other organisms – such as animals or decomposers – when they feed on the plant.

- Some of the energy is wasted, heating the soil and air.

Remember!
Both energy and carbon atoms are never destroyed or created. They are constantly being recycled around the planet.

B–A*

Genes and chromosomes

Chromosome numbers

- Chromosomes are long sections of DNA.

- Most human cells have 46 chromosomes, that is 23 from the gamete of each parent (sperm and egg), which carry about 25 000 genes.

- Each gene contains coded information that controls one characteristic. For example, some genes control hair colour. Other genes control eye colour.

- Most of these genes come in two or more forms. For example, a gene that controls hair colour might have one form that produces brown hair and a different form that produces red hair.

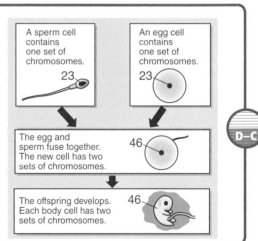

Figure 4: Chromosome numbers in gametes and other cells

Causes of variation

- Variation (differences) in organisms may be due to either: – the genes they have inherited (genetic causes) – the conditions in which they have developed (environmental causes) – or a combination of both.

B–A*

Improve your grade

Emma and Alice are identical twins. Emma has blonde hair and Alice has brown hair. Is this variation due to genetics or the environment? Explain your answer. **AO2 (2 marks)**

Reproduction

How it works

D–C

- In sexual reproduction, gametes and fertilisation are always involved.
- The new cell that is produced by fertilisation is a zygote. It divides repeatedly to produce a little ball of cells. This develops into an embryo and finally into an adult animal.
- Sexual reproduction produces variety in the offspring because each zygote has a different mix of genes from it parents and all its brothers and sisters.
- In asexual reproduction, an individual splits in two (as in bacteria) or a part divides off. This is the offspring.
- There is no variation. The new organisms all have exactly the same genes as their parent, and as each other. They are genetically identical (clones).

Remember!
Sexual reproduction does not always need two parents. Some plants have flowers that produce both male and female gametes, so they can fertilise themselves.

Different kinds of fertilisation

B–A*

- In birds and mammals, the male sperm are deposited and the egg is fertilised inside the female's body. This is called internal fertilisation.
- In other animals, such as fish, the male and female shed sperm and eggs into water. This is called external fertilisation. The fertilised eggs develop outside the female's body.

Cloning plants and animals

Cloning methods

D–C

- Taking cuttings is a way of making new plants from one original plant. Stems are cut from the parent plant; the ends dipped in hormone rooting powder and placed into soil. The cuttings will grow into new plants which are genetically identical to each other and the parent plant.
- Tissue culture can also be used to clone plants.
  - A small piece of tissue is taken from a root, stem or leaf of the parent plant. The tissue is then grown on a jelly containing all the nutrients it needs.
  - Everything has to be kept sterile, so this is usually done in a laboratory.
  - Eventually, each tiny group of cells grows into a complete adult plant.
- One technique to clone animals is called embryo transplants. This is sometimes done with farm animals, such as cows.
  - Egg cells are taken from a cow and fertilised with sperm from a bull.
  - One embryo is chosen and split into two (or more) and then each is placed into a host mother.
  - The calves born are clones of each other as they have the same genes.

Adult-cell cloning

B–A*

- Adult-cell cloning can be used to clone just one parent. Figure 1 shows how it is done.

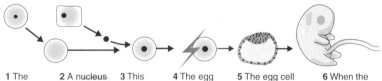

1 The nucleus is removed from an unfertilised egg cell.

2 A nucleus is taken from another cell in an adult animal's body.

3 This nucleus is put into the egg cell.

4 The egg cell is given a small electric shock. This persuades it to start dividing.

5 The egg cell grows into an embryo. Each of its cells contains exactly the same genes as the adult cell from which the nucleus was taken.

6 When the embryo is big enough, it is put into the uterus of a host mother, to continue its development.

Figure 1: Adult cell cloning

Improve your grade

Buttercup the cow produces the most milk in her herd. Her farmer is considering using her eggs for embryo transplants. Explain to him why cloning her might be an even better idea. **AO2 (3 marks)**

Genetic engineering

How it is done

- Bacteria have been genetically engineered to make human insulin. Figure 2 shows how this is done.

- Farmers spray bean fields with herbicides to kill weeds that compete with soya plants. The spray contains a chemical called glyphosate.

- Some soya bean varieties have been genetically engineered to give them a gene that makes them resistant to glyphosate.

- So when a farmer sprays the field with glyphosate, the weeds die but the bean plants do not.

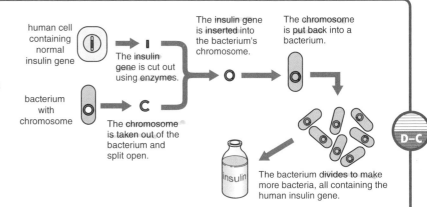

Figure 2: Bacteria have been genetically modified to produce human insulin

Genetic modification – good or bad?

- Some GM crop plants are resistant to attack by pests. This can greatly increase the yields and keep prices down. It also reduces the amount of pesticide that has to be sprayed.

- Some people have concerns about GM crops:
  - genes for a toxin to kill insects could be transferred to a wild plant, which could then disrupt natural food chains
  - there may be effects on humans of eating food from GM plants.

- GM crops have to be thoroughly tested before they are allowed to be grown on a large scale and there is no evidence that eating GM plants does any harm.

Evolution

Accepting Darwin's ideas

- Jean-Baptiste Lamarck suggested that changes in organisms caused by their environment were passed on to their offspring. We now know that this is not correct.

- Charles Darwin suggested that species gradually changed from one form to another by natural selection. Darwin thought that, in each generation, only the best-adapted individuals survive and reproduce to pass on their characteristics to the next generation.

- Darwin's ideas challenged the established thinking of the day, so his ideas were not accepted at first. They undermined the idea that God made all animals and plants.

- In the late 19th century, there was not much scientific evidence to support the theories of evolution and natural selection. At that time, no one even knew that genes existed, let alone the way that they are inherited. This was not discovered until 50 years later. However, this is the theory that almost all scientists today believe as there is now a lot of scientific evidence to support it.

Simple to complex?

- The very earliest forms of life on Earth were almost certainly simple, single-celled organisms. Today, many organisms are much more complicated. Does this mean that evolution produces increasingly complex organisms?

- Some bacteria living today are almost the same as bacteria that lived billions of years ago. They were, and still are, supremely well adapted to their environment.

Improve your grade

In 1859, Charles Darwin published a book containing his ideas about natural selection and evolution. Explain why many people at the time did not believe what it said. **AO2 (3 marks)**

Natural selection

How natural selection works

- This is how natural selection happens.
  - Living organisms produce many offspring.
  - The offspring vary from one another, because they have differences in their genes.
  - Some of them have genes that give them a better chance of survival. They are most likely to reproduce.
  - Their genes will be passed on to their offspring.
- Occasionally, unpredictable changes to chromosomes and genes, called mutations, happen.
- Occasionally, the new form of the gene increases an organism's chances of surviving and reproducing. It is therefore very likely to be passed on to the next generation. Over time, the new feature, produced by this gene, becomes more common in the species.
- The change in colour of the peppered moth from pale to dark is an example of evolution occurring because of a mutation.

> **EXAM TIP**
> You may be asked to explain how certain species evolved. Do this by applying the stages of natural selection: variation, competition, survival and reproduction.

The randomness of mutation

- Some forms of bacteria have become resistant to antibiotics.
- This happened as a result of mutation in the bacteria producing a form of a gene that helped them survive, even when the antibiotic was present in their environment.
- This was just chance. The bacteria did not purposefully mutate to become resistant.

Evidence for evolution

Comparing living organisms

- You can get clues about evolution by looking carefully at organisms that are alive today.
- For example, your arm, a bat's wing and a bird's wing all have the same bones in the same places. Similarities like this suggest that humans, bats and birds are quite closely related and that, long ago, an animal lived from which humans, bats and birds have all evolved (a common ancestor).
- Evolutionary trees like this one (Figure 1) show the pathway along which different kinds of organisms may have evolved.
- Organisms that lived longest ago are at the bottom of the tree.
- Models like this help to show how different groups of organisms might be related, which helps scientists to classify them.

Remember!
There are five main classification groups: bacteria, protoctists, fungi, plants and animals.

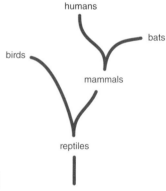

Figure 1: An evolutionary tree showing how humans, bats and birds are related

Classification

- Scientists are still discovering new species which change their ideas about how organisms should be classified.
- Recently, they have found that there are two distinct groups of these microorganisms. They are as different from one another as animals are from bacteria.
- They have now been split into two big groups – the bacteria and the archaea.

Improve your grade

The cheetah is the fastest land animal on Earth. It uses its speed to catch its prey. Use natural selection to explain how cheetahs have got faster over time. **AO2 (5 marks)**

Summary

To lose mass you need to use more energy than you take in. You can do this by eating less and exercising more. Metabolic rate is the speed at which energy is used by the body to carry out chemical reactions.

Keeping healthy

White blood cells attack pathogens via phagocytosis, antibodies and antitoxins. Vaccination encourages white blood cells to make antibodies against a pathogen. If the person is later infected, the antibodies will be made much more quickly. We say they are immune.

High blood cholesterol can lead to heart disease. It encourages the build-up of plaque which can lead to the blockage of arteries. Blood cholesterol level can be influenced by diet and inherited factors.

Antibiotics are drugs which kill bacteria. Some bacteria are becoming resistant to anti-biotics. An example is MRSA.

You can grow cultures of bacteria and fungi in liquids or jellies called a nutrient medium. It is important that everything is kept sterile.

Sensory neurones carry electrical impulses to the CNS from receptors. Motor neurones carry impulses from the CNS to effectors (muscles and glands) where they have an effect.

Nerves, hormones and drugs

Hormones control the menstrual cycle:
- FSH causes an egg to mature and the ovary to secrete oestrogen
- oestrogen causes the uterus lining to thicken and stops the production of FSH
- LH causes ovulation.

Conditions surrounding cells must be kept constant. These include water, sugar and salt concentration, and temperature. Sweating is one mechanism that the body uses to reduce body temperature when it rises above 37 °C.

Plant hormones called auxins cause their shoots to grow towards the light (positive phototropism) and roots to grow towards gravity (positive gravitropism). Artificial hormones can be used as rooting powder and herbicide.

Recreational drugs can be legal or illegal. Many drugs are addictive and can be dangerous if abused. Medicinal drugs have to be trialled before they can be prescribed by doctors.

Organisms have characteristics that enable them to live in their environment. This is called adaptation. The better the adaptation, the more likely it is that the organism will win the competition for resources and survive to reproduce.

Energy is wasted at each stage in a food chain, which results in less biomass at each trophic level. This is represented as a pyramid of biomass.

Interdependence and adaptation

Decay by microorganisms is an important way of recycling nutrients. The carbon cycle shows how carbon is moved around the planet.

Pollution levels can be monitored by measuring factors such as temperature and pH; or by studying the distribution of living pollution indicators, such as lichens to show air pollution and invertebrates to show water pollution.

Organisms vary because of the genes they inherit from their parents. Asexual reproduction results in clones. The offspring from sexual reproduction are different from their parents.

Genes and evolution

Genetic engineering means taking a gene from one organism, and putting it into another. This is used to make human insulin from bacteria and to create GM crops.

Scientists believe that all life on earth evolved from single-celled organisms that lived 3.5 billion years ago.

Clones can be created artificially by taking cuttings and carrying out tissue culture, embryo transplants and adult cell cloning.

Darwin's ideas about evolution explained how living things evolved due to variation and survival of the best adapted. Many people did not believe his ideas until 50 years after they were published.

Animal and plant cells

Cell organelles

- The different parts of a cell are called organelles. Each has a particular function.

- Figures 1 and 2 show the organelles you can see with a powerful light microscope.

EXAM TIP

Make sure you remember which organelles are found in both plant and animal cells and which are found only in plant cells. Figures 1 and 2 show you.

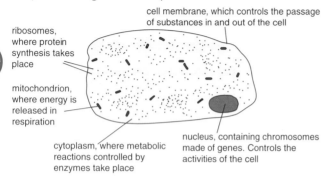

ribosomes, where protein synthesis takes place

cell membrane, which controls the passage of substances in and out of the cell

mitochondrion, where energy is released in respiration

cytoplasm, where metabolic reactions controlled by enzymes take place

nucleus, containing chromosomes made of genes. Controls the activities of the cell

Figure 1: An animal cell

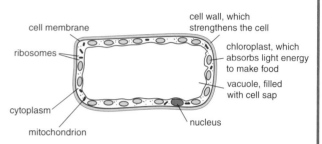

cell membrane

ribosomes

cytoplasm

mitochondrion

cell wall, which strengthens the cell

chloroplast, which absorbs light energy to make food

vacuole, filled with cell sap

nucleus

Figure 2: A plant cell

Electron microscopes

- Research laboratories use electron microscopes.

- They can magnify an object two million times. (A light microscope can only magnify by two thousand times.)

Microbial cells

Yeast, algae and bacteria

- Yeast is a single-celled fungus. Its cells have cell walls but they are not made of cellulose like plant cell walls. Fungi cannot photosynthesise as they have no chloroplasts.

- Algae are simple, plant-like organisms. Their cells are similar to plant cells.

- Bacteria do not have a nucleus. Their genes are in the cytoplasm.

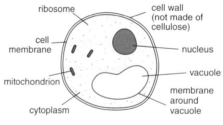

ribosome

cell membrane

mitochondrion

cytoplasm

cell wall (not made of cellulose)

nucleus

vacuole

membrane around vacuole

Figure 3: The structure of a yeast cell

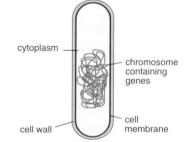

cytoplasm

chromosome containing genes

cell wall

cell membrane

Figure 4: The structure of a bacterial cell

Viruses

- Viruses are not made of cells. They do not have cell membranes, cytoplasm or a nucleus.
- Most viruses are made of a sphere of protein, with some DNA inside it.
- They are hundreds of times smaller than a cell.

Improve your grade

The image below was taken of some cells using a light microscope. State what type of cells they are and give reasons for your answer. **AO2 (2 marks)**

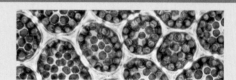

Diffusion

Cells and diffusion

- Diffusion is the spreading of the particles of a gas, or of any substance in solution, resulting in a net movement from a region where they are of a higher concentration, into a region where they are in a lower concentration.

- Most cells need oxygen so that they can respire. Oxygen diffuses into the cells from a higher concentration outside to a lower concentration inside.

- The concentration of oxygen inside a cell is kept low because the cell keeps on using it up.

Remember!
The speed of diffusion can be increased by increasing the difference in concentration (the concentration gradient) and increasing the temperature. (The faster that particles move around, the faster they will diffuse.)

A model cell

- Visking tubing contains millions of tiny holes which only let small molecules, like water, diffuse through. Large molecules, such as starch, cannot cross the membrane. We say it is partially permeable.

- This is similar to a cell membrane. Visking tubing can therefore be used as a model of a cell.

Specialised cells

Examples of specialised cells

- The human body contains hundreds of different kinds of specialised cells.

- Red blood cells, goblet cells and ciliated cells are just three of them.

EXAM TIP

Cells are measured in a unit called a micrometre, symbol µm. There are 1000 micrometres in one millimetre.

Goblet cells are found in the lining of the alimentary canal, and in the tubes leading down to the lungs. They make mucus, which helps food to slide easily through the alimentary canal, and helps to stop bacteria getting down into your lungs.

mucus that has been made by the cell

cell membrane

cytoplasm

nucleus

20 µm

Figure 5: Goblet cells

Specialised plant cells

- Root-hair cells are specialised plant cells.

- They are fine hair-like extensions of a root.

- Their large surface area enables plants to maximise their absorption of water from the soil.

Remember!
All the different types of specialised cell are the result of differentiation during the growth of the organism.

Improve your grade

Explain how a sperm cell is specialised.
AO2 (4 marks)

long tail with mitochondria is able to swim.

enzyme used to digest outside of the sperm allow nucleus to be fuse with

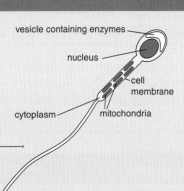

vesicle containing enzymes

nucleus

cell membrane

cytoplasm

mitochondria

30 µm

Tissues

Structure and function of tissues

- The cells that make up tissues are adapted for particular roles.
- Muscular tissue is specialised to produce movement.
- Glandular tissue is made up of cells which secrete (release) useful substances such as enzymes or hormones.

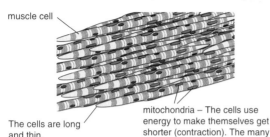

muscle cell

The cells are long and thin.

mitochondria – The cells use energy to make themselves get shorter (contraction). The many mitochondria in the cells provide the energy for contraction.

Figure 1: Muscular tissue

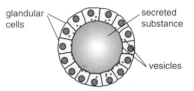

glandular cells

secreted substance

vesicles

The glandular cells contain many small vesicles of useful substances that the cell has made, such as enzymes or hormones. The substances are released outside the cell. This is called secretion.

Figure 2: Glandular cells

Single-celled and multicellular organisms

- Multicellular organisms have many different cells which are specialised for a particular function, an advantage over single-celled organisms.
- Some processes are easier for single-celled organisms, for example oxygen can easily diffuse into a single cell.
- Multicellular organisms need a transport system to bring oxygen to every cell in their body. They also have specialised tissues that are adapted for allowing things to move in and out of the body quickly.

Animal tissues and organs

Functions of the digestive system

- A system is a group of organs that performs a particular function.
- The function of the digestive system is to break down the food you eat so the food molecules can enter the blood.
- Each of the organs shown in Figure 3 has an important role in this.

Remember!

A group of cells is called a tissue. Organs are made up of different types of tissue. The heart contains muscle tissue that can contract and relax, nervous tissue to control the heart beat, and ligaments to hold the different tissues in place.

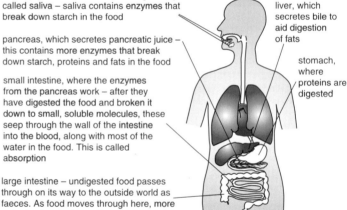

salivary glands, which secrete a digestive juice called saliva – saliva contains enzymes that break down starch in the food

pancreas, which secretes pancreatic juice – this contains more enzymes that break down starch, proteins and fats in the food

small intestine, where the enzymes from the pancreas work – after they have digested the food and broken it down to small, soluble molecules, these seep through the wall of the intestine into the blood, along with most of the water in the food. This is called absorption

large intestine – undigested food passes through on its way to the outside world as faeces. As food moves through here, more water is absorbed from it

liver, which secretes bile to aid digestion of fats

stomach, where proteins are digested

Figure 3: The functions of organs in the digestive system

Protecting the digestive system

- The whole of the digestive system is lined with epithelial tissue to protect the cells in the organs from digestive juices which could break them down.
- This tissue secretes large quantities of mucus, which forms a barrier over the inner surface of the digestive organs. The mucus also makes it easier for the food to slide through the digestive system.

Improve your grade

Describe why the stomach is classed as an organ. **AO2 (2 marks)**

Plant tissues and organs

Plant tissues

- The organs in a plant are made up of tissues.

- The whole plant is covered in a layer of epidermis. This helps to protect the underlying cells, stops the leaves from losing too much water and prevents pathogens from entering the plant.

- Most of the cells in a leaf are mesophyll cells. This is where photosynthesis takes place.

- Xylem and phloem tubes run through the entire plant.

- These are tubes which make up the plant's transport system: xylem carries water from the roots to the leaves; sugars are transported around the plant in phloem.

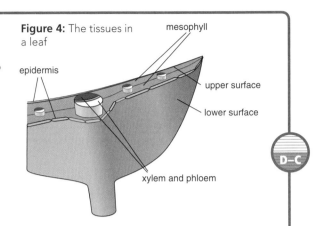

Figure 4: The tissues in a leaf

Remember!

Plant organs include roots, stem, flowers and leaves. Each is made up of tissues such as mesophyll, xylem and phloem.

Leaf epidermis

- The epidermal tissue on the lower surface of the leaf has little holes called stomata.

- These allow gases to diffuse into and out of the leaf.

Photosynthesis

Oxygen and energy for living things

- The word equation for photosynthesis is:

carbon dioxide + water $\xrightarrow{\text{energy from sunlight}}$ glucose + oxygen

- Millions of years ago there was hardly any oxygen in the air. Oxygen was first made when bacteria evolved that could photosynthesise. Gradually, over millions of years, the amount of oxygen in the air built up. Now more than 20 per cent of the air is oxygen. It has all been made by bacteria, algae and plants.

- In photosynthesis, light energy is stored in glucose molecules.

- The energy is transferred to animals when they eat the plants.

- Glucose can be converted into starch and stored for later use. Starch molecules are big and, unlike glucose, cannot diffuse out of cells.

> **EXAM TIP**
>
> The equation for photosynthesis shows us that water and carbon dioxide are reactants. Glucose and oxygen are products and are made from the rearrangement of the atoms in the reactants.

Chlorophyll and light absorption

- White light is a continuous spectrum of colours, from red to violet.

- Different parts of the spectrum have their own characteristic wavelengths. Short wavelength light looks blue and long wavelength light looks red.

- Light energy is absorbed by chlorophyll found in the chloroplasts of plant cells.

- Chlorophyll looks green because it absorbs the blue and red parts of the spectrum and reflects the green part.

◉ Improve your grade

Without photosynthesis, humans would not survive. Explain why. **AO2 (2 marks)**

Limiting factors

Limits to the speed of photosynthesis

D–C

- Figure 1 shows that as the light intensity increases, the rate of photosynthesis also increases.

- Light is a limiting factor for photosynthesis.

- However, there comes a point when the rate of photosynthesis does not increase any more, even when the plant is getting more light. This may be because it does not have enough carbon dioxide or the temperature is too low.

- A similarly shaped graph is produced when carbon dioxide in the air around a plant is increased.

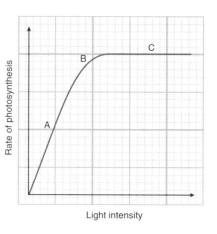

Figure 1: How light intensity affects the rate of photosynthesis

Greenhouses

B–A*

- Growing crops in a greenhouse gives the grower a lot of control over the conditions in which the plants live.

- A grower may be able to produce more tomatoes more quickly if they heat the greenhouse, but the cost of the fuel might outweigh the increase in what they are paid for the tomatoes.

Remember!

Light intensity, carbon dioxide concentration and temperature are all limiting factors for photosynthesis.

The products of photosynthesis

Mineral salts

D–C

- Glucose is made from carbon, hydrogen and oxygen atoms. Plants make other substances from glucose. These are shown in Table 1.

Table 1: Glucose products

Substance	Atoms the substance is made from			
	Carbon	Hydrogen	Oxygen	Nitrogen
carbohydrates	✓	✓	✓	
fats and oils	✓	✓	✓	
proteins	✓	✓	✓	✓

- To convert glucose into proteins, plants need nitrogen which they get in the form of mineral ions. They normally use nitrate ions, NO_3^-, and absorb them from the soil through their roots.

Choosing the storage product

B–A*

- Most plants store at least some energy as starch.
- Starch is a polymer made up of many glucose molecules linked together in a long chain.
- Unlike glucose, starch is insoluble. It forms grains inside cells, instead of dissolving and getting mixed up with everything else inside the cell.
- Fats and oils can store more energy per gram than starch but it is more difficult to make them and to break them down.

Improve your grade

Anna uses a fertiliser that is high in nitrates on her tomato plants. Explain why she does this. **AO2 (3 marks)**

Distribution of organisms

Factors affecting distribution

- Temperature: many species can live only in a particular temperature range.

- Availability of nutrients: very wet soils are usually short of nitrate ions, so only certain plants can live there. Animals can live only where their food is found.

- Amount of light: plants and algae must have light for photosynthesis. They cannot grow in really dark places.

- Availability of water: all organisms need water. Species that live in deserts have special adaptations that help them to obtain and conserve water. The seaweed egg wrack can only grow in places that are covered in water for most of the day or they get too hot and dry.

- Availability of oxygen and carbon dioxide: most organisms need oxygen, for respiration. They cannot live where oxygen is in short supply. Plants also need carbon dioxide, for photosynthesis.

 D–C

> **Remember!**
> Organisms can only live in environments for which they are adapted.

Interaction of physical and biotic factors

- The distribution of organisms is also affected by biotic factors – those involving other organisms, including competition and predation.

- If egg wrack grows low down on the shore, it is covered by water for most of the time. This means that sea-dwelling herbivorous animals can graze on it for a much longer part of the day.

- The egg wrack also has to compete for space and light with other seaweeds that are better adapted for growing in deep water.

B–A*

Using quadrats to sample organisms

valid result => randomly

Using quadrats

- Quadrats can be used to measure the distribution of organisms in a habitat. It is best to place the quadrats randomly. Once you have placed your quadrat, you need to identify each species inside it.

- Then you can either:
  - count the numbers of each one
  - estimate the percentage of the area inside the quadrat that each species occupies.

- You should repeat this process many times. Work out the mean number of, or area covered by, each species.

- A transect is used to find out if the distribution of organisms changes as you move from one habitat to another.

(a) counting individuals within a quadrat

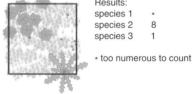

Results:
species 1   *
species 2   8
species 3   1

* too numerous to count

(b) estimating percentage cover in a quadrat

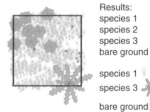

Results:
species 1   60%
species 2   20%
species 3   10%
bare ground   10%

species 1   species 2
species 3
bare ground

Figure 2: Two ways of collecting data from a quadrat

D–C

EXAM TIP

Placing the quadrat randomly ensures the results are valid. Placing the quadrat in at least 10 different places and calculating the mean will increase reliability.

Choosing quadrat size

- One way of finding the optimum size for a quadrat is to try out different sizes, and then count how many different species you find in each size.

- Choose the one that is able to contain at least one organism from each species that lives in the habitat you are sampling.

 B–A*

Improve your grade

Simon went on holiday to Mexico. He noticed that the plants growing there were very different to the plants growing at home in the UK. Explain the reasons for this difference in distribution. **AO2 (3 marks)**

Proteins

Protein shapes

- Each protein molecule is made of a very long chain of hundreds of amino acids linked together.

amino acid
Figure 1: The structure of part of a protein molecule

- The type and order of the amino acids determines the shape of the protein. The shape of a protein molecule affects the way it behaves.

- Some protein molecules, like those in muscles, make long, thin fibres.

- Enzymes, antibodies and hormones usually have a globular (ball-like) structure, which often has a dent in it that is a perfect fit for one other kind of molecule. For example, an antibody molecule might have a dent that perfectly fits a particular molecule on a particular bacterium.

Making proteins in the body

- Animals make proteins from the amino acids they get from food.

- During digestion, protein molecules are broken down into amino acids. These are then absorbed through the wall of the small intestine and are carried all over the body in the blood. Each cell takes up the amino acids that it needs from the blood. Inside the cell, on ribosomes, amino acids are linked together to make the particular kinds of proteins that the cell requires.

> **Remember!**
> There are 20 different amino acids. The body can make all the different proteins it needs from these amino acids by arranging them in different orders.

- The genes in the nucleus provide instructions about exactly which amino acids to link together, and in which order.

Enzymes

Factors affecting enzyme activity

- An enzyme molecule is **a long** chain of **amino acids**, folded into a ball. There is a dent in the ball into which another molecule can fit. This dent is the active site of the enzyme.

- The molecule that fits into the enzyme is called its substrate. The enzyme makes the substrate react, changing it into a new substance.

- Most of the enzymes in the body work best at about 37 °C, which is normal body temperature. This is their optimum temperature. At temperatures above the optimum, the enzyme begins to uncurl and lose its shape. Once the active site has lost its shape, the substrate no longer fits.

- When the enzyme is permanently changed in this way, it is said to be denatured.

- Enzymes are also sensitive to pH. If the pH is a long way from the enzyme's optimum pH, then the enzyme denatures.

How temperature affects enzymes

- Figure 2 shows how temperature affects enzyme activity.

- When the temperature is low, the enzyme and its substrate are both moving slowly. They do not bump into each other very often. When they do collide, there is not very much energy involved, so the substrate may not react.

- As temperature increases, the molecules move more quickly so there is more chance that they will collide and react.

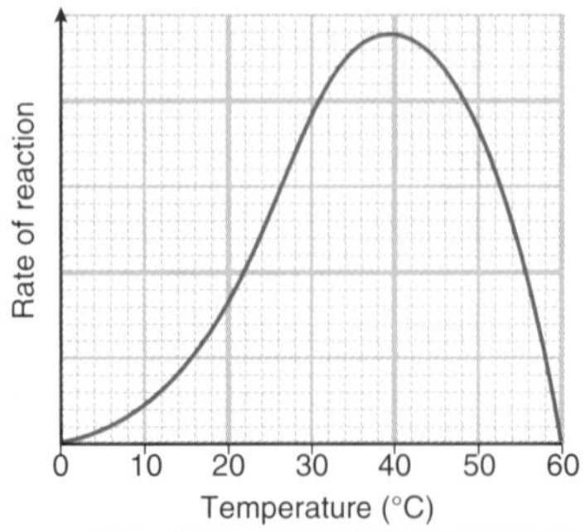

Figure 2: How temperature affects enzyme activity

(graph: Rate of reaction vs Temperature (°C), x-axis marked 0, 10, 20, 30, 40, 50, 60)

Improve your grade

Pepsin is an enzyme that helps break down proteins in the stomach. It has an optimum pH of 2. Use this information to explain why the stomach produces hydrochloric acid. **AO2 (2 marks)**

Enzymes and digestion

Types of enzymes

- Digestive enzymes pass out of cells in glandular tissue, go into the space inside the gut and become mixed up with the food.

- They cut large food molecules into smaller bits.

- There are three main groups of digestive enzymes (see Table 1).

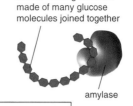

starch – a long molecule made of many glucose molecules joined together

sugar molecules – small enough to pass through the gut wall and into the blood

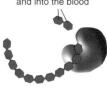

amylase

Figure 3: How amylase digests starch

	Substrate	Product	Where enzyme is produced
amylase	starch	sugars	salivary glands in the mouth and pancreas
protease	protein	amino acids	pancreas, stomach and small intestine
lipase	lipids (fats and oils)	fatty acids and glycerol	pancreas and small intestine

Table 1: The main groups of digestive enzymes

Acid and alkali

- The liver produces bile, which is stored in the gall bladder. When food arrives in the small intestine, bile flows along the bile duct and mixes with the food.

- Bile is an alkali. It neutralises the acid from the stomach. This provides the slightly alkaline pH which is the optimum pH for the enzymes in the small intestine.

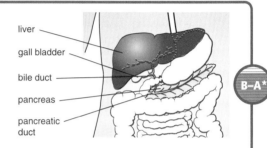

liver

gall bladder

bile duct

pancreas

pancreatic duct

Figure 4: Bile is produced in the liver

Enzymes at home

Biological detergents

- Biological washing powders (detergents) contain lipase and protease enzymes.

- Some stains on clothes – for example blood stains – cannot be removed using ordinary detergents. The enzymes help to break down the stains into substances that dissolve in water. The stains can then wash away.

- The enzymes in detergents often work best at about 30 °C.

Skin complaints

- Some stains on clothes, like blood, are made up of proteins. The proteases in detergents change the proteins into small, soluble amino acid molecules. These can easily be washed away.

How Science Works

- In the 1970s, doctors began to notice many more patients with sore skin on their hands. The knowledge that the new biological detergents contained proteases that could break down skin protein (keratin) led many to link their use to the sore skin. Research has failed to confirm this idea. However, many people still report that their skin is sensitive to biological detergents.

Improve your grade

Dipesh mixed some starch with amylase in a beaker and left the mixture in a water bath at 37 °C. After 30 minutes, he tested the mixture to see if there was any starch present. Predict what he will find and give a reason for your answer. **AO2 (2 marks)**

Enzymes in industry

Baby foods, sugar syrup and slimming foods

- Baby foods: In young babies, the digestive system is not fully developed. Some baby food manufacturers add proteases to their products. These enzymes break down large protein molecules into amino acids. When the baby eats this pre-digested food, it can absorb the amino acids.

- Sugar syrup: This is used in making sweets and sports drinks. Starch solution is easy to make by cooking potatoes or maize and mixing them with water. The starch can then be changed into sugar syrup by adding carbohydrase enzymes such as amylase.

- Slimming foods: These often contain a very sweet sugar called fructose instead of glucose. Fructose is made from glucose using an enzyme called isomerase.

Making soft-centre chocolates

- A mixture of sucrose, flavouring, colouring and an enzyme called sucrase are mixed together to make a paste.

- The paste is moulded, left to set then liquid chocolate is poured over it.

- The chocolates are then warmed up a little, so that the enzyme begins to work on the sucrose inside them.

- The following chemical reaction happens inside the chocolate case:
  sucrose → glucose + fructose

- The mixture of glucose and fructose makes thick, soft syrup inside the chocolates.

Aerobic respiration

Releasing energy

- Most of the time, cells release energy by combining glucose molecules with oxygen. This is called aerobic respiration.

- The word equation is:
  glucose + oxygen → carbon dioxide + water (+ energy)

- Your body obtains oxygen from the air which enters your blood in your lungs. It is transported in the blood to all your body cells. The carbon dioxide that the cells make is carried back, in the blood, to the lungs.

- Aerobic respiration takes place in the mitochondria of cells.

- They contain all the enzymes that are needed to make the reactions of respiration happen quickly.

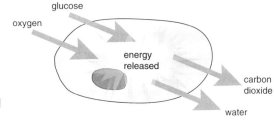

Figure 1: Aerobic respiration

Respiration and photosynthesis

- Photosynthesis locks up energy from sunlight inside glucose molecules. Respiration releases this energy so that cells can use it.
- When there is sunlight, mesophyll cells in plant leaves are photosynthesising and respiring.
- Both reactions are happening at once – photosynthesis in their chloroplasts and respiration in their mitochondria.
- In bright light, photosynthesis happens a lot faster than respiration.
- At night, photosynthesis stops, but the cells carry on respiring.

EXAM TIP

Notice that the chemical equation for aerobic respiration is the same as the one for photosynthesis but in reverse. This means that if you only learn one for the exam, you will also know the other.

Improve your grade

Explain why breathing rate increases when you exercise. **AO2 (3 marks)**

Using energy

Using the energy

- Building large molecules: Cells use energy to make small molecules join together to make long chains.

- Muscle contraction: Muscles use energy to contract. They contain a store of glucose called glycogen, which is made up of many glucose molecules linked together. When a muscle needs energy, it breaks down the glycogen to produce glucose for use in respiration.

- Maintaining a steady body temperature: Mammals and birds keep their body temperature around 37 °C. If their environment is colder than they are, then heat is lost from their body. Respiration in cells releases energy, which increases body temperature.

- Making amino acids: Plants can make amino acids from sugar and nitrate ions. This requires energy.

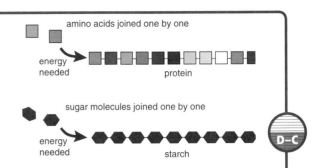

Figure 2: Linking molecules together requires energy

Energy for swimming

- Sperm cells are packed full of mitochondria. These produce energy to drive its tail movements so it can swim towards the egg (a distance of 15 cm).

- They do not have any food reserves such as glycogen. Instead, they use sugars from the fluid in which they were ejected from the male.

Anaerobic respiration

Lactic acid and oxygen debt

- Anaerobic respiration is incomplete breakdown of glucose to lactic acid: glucose → lactic acid (+ a little energy)

- It releases far less energy than aerobic respiration (aerobic releases 16.1 kJ per gram of glucose, anaerobic only releases 0.8 kJ).

- Lactic acid builds up in the muscles. It makes muscles feel tired and can cause cramps. They stop contracting efficiently.

- After you have stopped exercising you have to get rid of this lactic acid.

- You continue to breathe heavily. This takes in the extra oxygen that you need to get rid of the lactic acid (the oxygen debt).

Remember!
Anaerobic respiration is carried out whenever your body cannot get an adequate supply of oxygen to the cells.

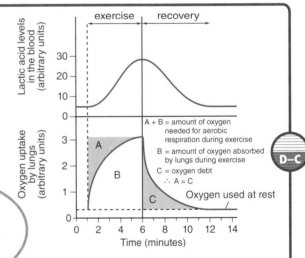

Figure 3: Anaerobic respiration, lactic acid and oxygen debt

Maximum oxygen uptake

- When you exercise, your muscles use more oxygen so you breathe more deeply and more quickly. Your heart beats faster so that oxygenated blood is pumped to your active muscles more quickly.

- The maximum volume of oxygen that your body is able to use per minute is called VO_2 max. The fitter you are, the higher the value of your VO_2 max.

Improve your grade

You are involved in a race. At first you sprint off feeling full of energy. However, halfway through, your legs start to ache and you have to stop. Explain why this happened. **AO2 (3 marks)**

Cell division – mitosis

Mitosis and chromosomes

D–C

- More cells are made when existing cells divide into two. This is mitosis.
- Mitosis is very important because it provides cells for growth and to replace dead or damaged cells.
- Normal body cells have 23 **pairs** of chromosomes.
- Before a cell divides by mitosis, it first copies each chromosome.
- When the cell divides by mitosis, the chromosomes are shared out equally between the two new cells.

1 Before mitosis begins, each chromosome is copied exactly. The two copies stay attached to one another.

2 During mitosis, the two copies of each chromosome move apart.

3 When the cell divides, each new cell has two complete sets of chromosomes. The two new cells are genetically identical.

Figure 1: Before and during mitosis

How mitosis happens

B–A*

- Mitosis happens in the following stages.
  - Chromosomes are copied and line up along the middle of the cell.
  - The identical copies of each chromosome split apart and move to opposite ends of the cell.
  - The chromosomes now form into two nuclei.
  - New cell membranes form and two new cells have been made.

Cell division – meiosis

Meiosis and chromosomes

D–C

- Before meiosis happens, the chromosomes in the cell that is going to divide are copied. This is just the same as in mitosis.
- Then the cell divides. Unlike in mitosis, it **divides twice.** This means that four cells are produced – not two, as happens in mitosis.
- Each of the new cells gets only half the original number of chromosomes.
- Figure 2 shows what happens when a cell divides by meiosis.

1 Before meiosis begins, each chromosome is copied exactly. The two copies stay attached to one another.

2 Each chromosome finds its partner from the other set.

3 The chromosomes separate from their partners, and the cell divides.

4 Each cell divides again, this time separating the two copies of each chromosome.

5 Four new cells have been produced, each with a single set of chromosomes.

Figure 2: Before and during meiosis

Comparing mitosis and meiosis

B–A*

- Table 1 shows the differences between meiosis and mitosis.

Table 1: Comparing mitosis and meiosis

Mitosis	Meiosis
The cell divides once.	The cell divides twice.
Two cells are made.	Four cells are made.
The new cells have the **same** number of chromosomes as the original cell.	The new cells have **half** the number of chromosomes as the original cell.
This is how new body cells are made.	This is how **gametes** are made.
It happens in **all** parts of the body.	It happens **only** in the **testes** and **ovaries.**

EXAM TIP

It is easy to get mitosis and meiosis mixed up. Remember that meiosis is the process that produces gametes (sex cells). An easy way to remember is that meiosis contains an *e* for egg and an *s* for sperm.

Improve your grade

Explain why mitosis is an essential process in the formation of a baby from a fertilised egg. **AO2 (2 marks)**

mitosis needed to produce the egg, to embryo

Stem cells

Embryo and adult stem cells

- In animals, the fertilised egg divides over and over again to produce an embryo. For the first few days, all of these cells stay as stem cells. Each one has the potential to develop into any kind of cell in the human body.

- Most cells differentiate and form specialised cells. A few remain as stem cells and can continue to divide and specialise throughout adult life.

- In plants, many cells can differentiate at any time during their lives.

- Stem cells from embryos and adults (particularly bone marrow stem cells) could be used to replace damaged tissues in the future.

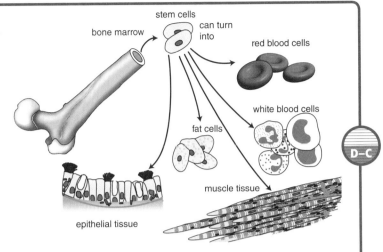

Figure 3: Bone marrow stem cells can produce many different kinds of specialised cells

Stem cells for the future

- 'Stem cell cures' are being sold over the internet. Most of these have never been tested, do not work and are potentially dangerous.

- It is important that patients are protected from these untested treatments but it is also important that trials are carried out as they could lead to success.

Genes, alleles and DNA

Alleles and DNA fingerprinting

- Most genes come in several different forms, called alleles. For example, a gene for hair colour might have one allele that gives black hair, another which gives brown hair, another which gives red hair and so on.

- Humans have two sets of chromosomes in each cell – one from each parent.

- There is a gene for the same characteristic at the same place on the same chromosome in each set. The two genes might be the same allele or different alleles.

- Everybody's DNA is slightly different.

- Forensic scientists often use DNA from cells in fluids, hair or bones to identify a body, or to identify a person who was at the scene of the crime. They make a DNA fingerprint by cutting up a sample of DNA into little pieces to form a series of stripes. Each person's pattern of stripes is unique.

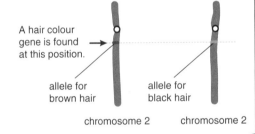

Figure 4: Genes have different forms, called alleles

Analysing your DNA

- Scientists are now able to link certain alleles with an increased risk of getting some diseases.

- There are now several commercial companies who will analyse your DNA and tell you which diseases you might develop later in your life.

⊙ Improve your grade

In the future, we may be able to use an individual's genome to calculate the likelihood of them developing certain diseases such as cancer. Evaluate this potential application. **AO2 (6 marks)**

Mendel

Mendel's experiments

D–C

- Mendel pollinated peas with purple flowers with pollen from white flowers. All the offspring had purple flowers. Mendel then tried breeding these together. He found that the offspring were a mixture of purple and white.

- He decided that:
  - each plant must have two 'factors' for flower colour
  - the purple factors were 'stronger' than the white factors
  - each factor must be separately inherited, that is, the factors did not 'blend' together.

- Mendel presented his findings to other scientists in 1865. At that time no one knew anything about how cells divided or that chromosomes and genes existed. It was not until after Mendel died in 1900 that other scientists rediscovered his work. Today, we know that Mendel's 'factors' are alleles of genes.

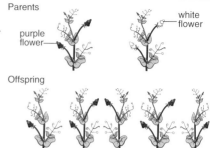

Figure 1: The result of crossing purple flowered pea plants with white flowered pea plants

Luck or good judgement?

B–A*

- Mendel was lucky with his experiments. By chance – or perhaps good judgement – he picked on characteristics that never do 'blend' together.

- There are many other features that do 'blend' together. For example, with some other kinds of flowers, if you cross red ones with white ones, you obtain pink ones.

How genes affect characteristics

Alleles come in pairs

D–C

- In rabbits, there might be a gene for fur colour: one allele of the gene may give black fur, another allele may give white fur.

- In a rabbit's cells, there are two complete sets of chromosomes. This means that there are two copies of each gene.

- If you call the allele for black fur B, and the allele for white fur b, then there are three possible combinations: BB, Bb or bb.

- Bb produces black fur. This is because the B allele is dominant. The b allele is recessive.

- When a dominant and a recessive allele are together, only the dominant one has an effect.

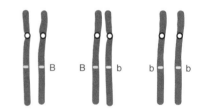

Figure 2: The three possible combinations of alleles for fur colour in a rabbit's cells

Figure 3: A rabbit with black fur could have the alleles BB or Bb. A rabbit with white fur can only have the alleles bb

BB　　Bb　　bb

Intersex conditions

B–A*

- Sex is determined by a pair of chromosomes called the sex chromosomes. Males are XY, females are XX.
- Around 1 in 100 people have some characteristics of both sexes (intersex conditions) caused by a zygote ending up with a combination such as XXY or XYY or even just a single X chromosome.
- Usually, if at least one Y chromosome is present, the person develops as a male, because it is the Y chromosome that determines maleness.

Improve your grade

Katy has red hair. Both her parents have brown hair. Explain how Katy inherited red hair when her parents do not have it. **AO2 (3 marks)**

Inheriting chromosomes and genes

Genetic diagrams for alleles of genes

- Genetic diagrams are used to show how alleles of genes are inherited.

- Figure 4 shows the outcome of a male rabbit with alleles Bb for fur colour breeding with a female with bb.

- Half of the sperm cells will have allele B and the other half will have allele b.

- All of the female's eggs will contain allele b.

- The genetic diagram shows you to expect about half of the baby rabbits to have the alleles Bb and have black fur. The other half would be bb and have white fur.

- It is important to remember that a genetic diagram only shows chances, not the actual results of the cross.

Parents	male rabbit with black hair	female rabbit with white hair
	Bb	bb
Gametes	Ⓑ and Ⓑ	all Ⓑ

Offspring

	Ⓑ	Ⓑ
all Ⓑ	Bb black	bb white

Figure 4: Rabbit fur colour

Remember!

It is usually a good idea to complete a genetic diagram by summarising the approximate chances of getting each of the different genotypes and phenotypes. In the above cross, the expected genotype ratio is 1Bb : 1bb.

Test crosses

- If an organism has a characteristic that is controlled by a dominant allele, then there are two possible combinations of alleles that it might have.

- The only way to find out which one you'll get is by doing a breeding experiment. This is a test cross.

EXAM TIP

If you are asked to draw a genetic diagram make sure you include the whole sequence of descriptions, not just the square showing the gametes and offspring.

B–A*

How genes work

DNA and protein synthesis

- A gene is a length of DNA that carries the code for making one protein.

- Each strand of a DNA molecule is made up of a **sequence of four bases**.

- The sequence of bases in the DNA determines the sequence of amino acids in the protein that is made.

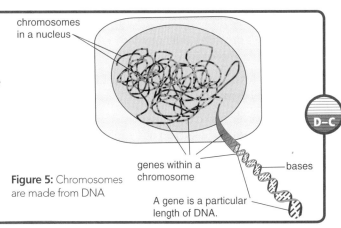

chromosomes in a nucleus

genes within a chromosome

bases

A gene is a particular length of DNA.

Figure 5: Chromosomes are made from DNA

Mutations

- Mutations in DNA form new alleles of genes.

- Many people have a slightly **different version** of the haemoglobin gene. It differs by only **one base** in the DNA but it is enough to cause a serious condition called sickle cell anaemia.

- In conditions where oxygen is in short supply (such as when doing a lot of exercise), it makes the red blood cells go so badly out of shape that they clump together and get stuck in blood capillaries.

Improve your grade

The height of pea plants is controlled by a single gene. The tall allele is dominant. A tall pea plant was bred with a short pea plant. The offspring formed was in the ratio 1 tall : 1 short. Draw a genetic diagram to show the cross. **AO2 (4 marks)**

Genetic disorders

How they are inherited

- Polydactyly is a condition in which a person has more than five fingers on their hands, or more than five toes on their feet.

- It is caused by a dominant allele, so you only need to inherit one allele in order to have this condition.

- Figure 1 shows how polydactyly was inherited in one family.

- Cystic fibrosis is a disorder of cell membranes and affects the lungs and pancreas.

- It is caused by a recessive allele.

- A person with the disorder will have two recessive alleles. Someone with one recessive allele is called a carrier.

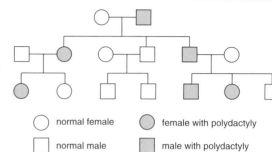

Figure 1: Example of a family tree for polydactyly

Remember!
Carriers of cystic fibrosis will not have any symptoms of the illness. They may not even know they are a carrier unless they pass this allele on and have a child with cystic fibrosis.

Embryo screening

- Parents who know they are carriers for a serious genetic disease may choose to have a child by IVF so the embryos can be screened.

- This involves testing the embryos' DNA to find out if any have the alleles, then only implanting the unaffected ones into the mother's uterus.

Fossils

The fossil record

- Fossils provide evidence which suggests that all species of living things that exist today have evolved from simple life-forms.

- The fossil record for most species is incomplete because most organisms do not form fossils when they die (they decay instead).

- However, there are a number of ways that the remains of plants and animals can be preserved as fossils.
  - Bones and teeth do not easily decay.
  - Some parts of organisms do not decay because conditions are not suitable for decay organisms.
  - Parts of an organism may be replaced by other materials such as hard minerals as they decay.
  - Traces of an organism, like footprints, may be preserved in rocks as prints.

- The fossil record for some organisms, such as the horse, is complete and shows how it has evolved over the last 50–60 million years.

How did life evolve?

- There is not enough valid or reliable evidence to be certain how life on Earth first evolved.
- Some scientists think that life first evolved in the seas, from the mix of chemicals that was present on the early Earth.
- All living things on Earth contain a genetic code in their DNA.
- This is a very strong piece of evidence that all life on Earth has evolved from the same common ancestors.

Improve your grade

Polydactyly is caused by a dominant allele. Jessica has polydactyly. Ryan does not have it. Could their children have polydactyly? Explain your answer. **AO2 (3 marks)**

Extinction

Causes of extinction

- Life on Earth began about 3.8 billion years ago. As Earth slowly changed, many different plants and animal species became extinct (died out) and were replaced by new types.

- There are several causes of extinction:
  - a change in the environment – for example, the temperature might increase and so individuals that cannot adapt or move away will die out
  - new predators – may cause the extinction of species that are its prey and are not adapted to get away
  - new diseases – if a new, fatal, disease is introduced to a habitat then the species living there may not have immunity and so will die
  - a more successful competitor – if there is a limited amount of food in a habitat and two different species are competing for it, the less well-adapted one may become extinct.

Remember!
If a species is not able to quickly adapt to new situations it may become extinct.

D–C

Mass extinctions

- The fossil record suggests that there have been several periods in Earth's history when huge numbers of species became extinct over a relatively short period of time.

- It is thought that these were probably caused when a sudden, catastrophic event produced massive changes on Earth.

B–A*

New species

How new species arise

- Many new species arise through a series of steps. Here is an example.

1 Geographical isolation
A few lizards drift away from the mainland on a floating log and end up on an island. They are isolated from the rest of the species.

2 Genetic variation
In both the mainland lizards and the island lizards, there are many different alleles of genes which lead to variation.

3 Natural selection
The environment, predators, etc on the mainland are different from those on the island. Natural selection takes place and different features are selected for.

4 Speciation
Over time, more and more differences build up between the two populations of lizards until they are no longer the same species.

Remember!
Biologists define a species as a group of organisms that share similar characteristics, and that can breed together to produce fertile offspring.

D–C

Other kinds of isolation

- Geographic isolation is not the only way that two populations of the same species can become isolated.

- Any situation that forces members of the same species to start breeding within selected groups can cause a new species to arise.

- For example, one kind of fruit fly can breed on either apples or hawthorn fruits. It seems that those that hatched on apples always go back to apples to breed, while those that hatched on hawthorn fruits always go back to hawthorn fruits.

B–A*

Improve your grade

Around 300 years ago, the dodo lived on the island of Mauritius. It had no predators. People arrived on the island. They brought predators such as dogs, pigs and rats. Explain why the dodo became extinct. **AO2 (2 marks)**

B2 Summary

Cells, tissues and organs

The parts of cells are called organelles. Each has an important part to play in the function of the cell.

Plant, animal and microbial cells have many similarities and some differences.

Oxygen and other dissolved substances move into and out of cells by diffusion.

In animals and plants, cells are grouped into tissues. Organs are made up of different tissues working together to carry out a function.

Different types of cells have different structures which enable them to carry out their specific functions. They are specialised.

Plants and the environment

Chlorophyll in plant cells absorbs energy from sunlight. This energy is used to convert carbon dioxide and water to glucose and oxygen in a reaction called photosynthesis.

The distribution of different species of organism in the environment is affected by physical factors. These include temperature, nutrients, light, water, oxygen and carbon dioxide.

Limiting factors, including light, temperature and carbon dioxide concentration, affect the rate of photosynthesis.

Glucose is used to supply energy; to make cellulose for cell walls; to make storage substances like starch and fats; and to make protein to build new cells and enzymes.

Quantitative data about the distribution of organisms can be collected using quadrats and transects.

Proteins and respiration

Protein molecules are long chains of amino acids. Hormones, antibodies and enzymes are all proteins.

Enzymes are biological catalysts which control all metabolic reactions, including digestion. They are also used in the home and in industry.

All living organisms release energy from glucose by respiration.

The rate at which enzymes work is affected by temperature and pH.

In aerobic respiration, energy is released when glucose is combined with oxygen. During exercise, when muscles are using a lot of energy, heart rate and breathing rate increase to provide muscles with extra oxygen.

In anaerobic respiration, a small amount of energy is released from glucose without using oxygen.

Cell division, inheritance and speciation

Cells normally divide by mitosis, which results in two genetically identical daughter cells. To produce gametes, cells divide by meiosis, which produces genetically different cells, each with half the normal number of chromosomes.

Clones can be created artificially by taking cuttings and carrying out tissue culture, embryo transplants and adult cell cloning.

New species can arise if two populations of a species become separated. Natural selection may result in them becoming so different that they can no longer interbreed.

Genes are passed from one generation to the next. A gene controlling a particular characteristic may have different forms, called alleles. Some diseases, such as cystic fibrosis, can be inherited.

Genetic diagrams can be used to predict the probable characteristics of the offspring of two parents.

Fossils provide evidence about some of the species that lived long ago.

Osmosis

What is osmosis?

- Osmosis is the movement of water from a dilute solution to a concentrated solution through a partially permeable membrane. It is a type of diffusion.

- Partially permeable membranes let through small molecules like water, but not larger molecules like glucose (sugar). Cell membranes are partially permeable.

- Visking tubing is partially permeable and can be used to demonstrate osmosis.

Remember!
Osmosis is a type of diffusion, but it is only the movement of water molecules.

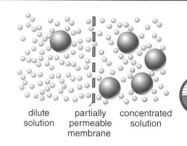

dilute solution partially permeable membrane concentrated solution

Figure 1: Explaining osmosis

Key ○ water molecule ● sugar molecule

D–C

Why does osmosis happen?

- Osmosis happens because of the random movement of molecules. In a liquid of sugar solution, all of the molecules are moving.

- If molecules bump into the walls of the membrane they will bounce away; if they bump into a hole in the wall, then water is small enough to move through the membrane whilst sugar molecules are too big and bounce back.

- The more dilute the solution, the more water there is. So in a dilute solution there is a greater chance of water molecules bumping into a hole and passing through the membrane into the more concentrated solution.

- If we know the concentrations on either side of the membrane, we can predict that the water will always flow towards the more concentrated solution.

- Sports drinks are isotonic, this means they are the same concentration as blood should be.

- They contain sucrose to replace that used in respiration; and water and ions to replace that lost in sweat.

B–A*

Osmosis and cells

Effects of osmosis in cells

- When an animal cell is placed in a solution that is more dilute than the cytoplasm, water enters the cell by osmosis and the cell bursts.

- When an animal cell is placed in a solution that is more concentrated than the cytoplasm, water leaves the cell by osmosis and the cell shrinks.

- When a plant cell is placed in a solution that is more dilute than the cytoplasm, water moves into the cell by osmosis and the cell membrane pushes against the cell wall.

- When a plant cell is placed in a solution that is more concentrated than the cytoplasm, water moves out of the cell by osmosis and the cell membrane pulls away from the cell wall.

D–C

Osmosis and plant cells

- The cell wall in plants prevents them from bursting in dilute solutions, this means that plants such as potatoes can be used to demonstrate osmosis.

- The cell wall also stops plants from collapsing if they don't have enough water. If the cell membrane has pulled away from the cell wall, the cell wall is strong enough to maintain the shape of the cell.

B–A*

Improve your grade

Iodine turns starch a blue-black colour. The diagram shows what happens when starch is put into visking tubing and placed into a beaker of water containing iodine. Explain why the water remains brown but inside the visking tubing it is blue-black.
AO2 and 3 (2 marks)

concentrated sugar solution

dilute sugar solution

Visking tubing – a partially permeable membrane

starch molecules too big
only water can diffuse through
ppm.
from high conc (outside), to low conc (inside)

Active transport

What is active transport?

D–C

- Active transport is a type of transport that requires energy.
- Unlike diffusion, active transport moves molecules against the concentration gradient.
- Molecules are moved from a dilute solution to a concentrated solution.
- The energy needed comes from cell respiration.
- Active transport is used by root cells to absorb minerals, like nitrates, from dilute concentrations in the soil.

absorption from glucose.

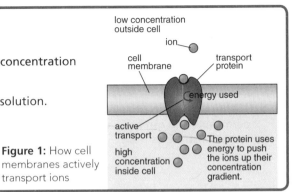

Figure 1: How cell membranes actively transport ions

low concentration outside cell

ion

cell membrane

transport protein

energy used

active transport

high concentration inside cell

The protein uses energy to push the ions up their concentration gradient.

How does active transport happen?

B–A*

- Special proteins in the cell membrane transport the molecules from the surroundings into the cell.
- Cell respiration occurs in the mitochondria, where glucose is broken down and combined with oxygen to release energy.
- Cells that do a lot of active transport, like root hair cells, have lots of mitochondria.
- To obtain the oxygen needed for respiration to fuel the active transport, root hair cells absorb oxygen from the air spaces in the soil.

Remember!
If the transport is against the concentration gradient, energy is needed.

Exchange surfaces

Where are exchange surfaces?

D–C

- Exchange surfaces are used for taking in substances from the surroundings and getting rid of other substances.
- Exchange surfaces are found in the lungs, intestines and kidneys.
- The small intestine has villi to absorb nutrients from food into the blood.
- The lungs have alveoli to absorb oxygen from the air and to release carbon dioxide from the blood.
- The kidneys have nephrons which get rid of urea from the blood.
- Exchange surfaces are adapted for efficient exchange including:
  - large surface areas, e.g. villi in the small intestine
  - small distances for diffusion, e.g. flattened cells in alveoli
  - movement to maintain concentration gradients, e.g. pumping the blood through nephrons.

Adaptations of exchange surfaces

B–A*

- The small intestine is specially adapted for exchange by having:
  - villi (folds in the intestine lining) that increase surface area
  - thin walls so there is a small distance for diffusion
  - proteins for active transport to absorb nutrients against their concentration gradient
  - a dense network of blood capillaries to move the nutrients away to maintain the concentration gradient.

capillary

some substances taken up by active transport – against the concentration gradient

some substances taken up by diffusion – down the concentration gradient

Figure 2: How a villus absorbs nutrients

blood in   blood out

⊙ Improve your grade

If people with Coeliac disease eat wheat, their villi can be damaged and become flattened. How and why would this effect the absorption of nutrients? **AO2 (2 marks)**

 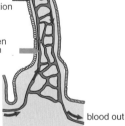

smaller surface area,   of gas exchange rate breathing harder

Gas exchange

What is gas exchange?

- Gas exchange occurs when oxygen diffuses into the blood and carbon dioxide diffuses into the air.
- It happens in the alveoli in the lungs.
- There are thousands of alveoli, which increases the surface area of the lungs.
- To reach the alveoli, air passes through the trachea, bronchi and bronchioles.
- The alveoli and the capillaries are one cell thick, so there's a short diffusion distance.
- Movement of the blood, and ventilation, maintain the concentration gradients needed for diffusion.

D–C

Surface area to volume ratio

- To maintain the concentration gradients needed for diffusion, the diaphragm and the intercostal muscles contract and relax to exchange air.
- Single-celled organisms have a large surface area to volume ratio, so they don't need a ventilation system: they have enough surface area on their cell membrane to exchange gases.
- Multicellular organisms have a small surface area to volume ratio, so need specially adapted gas-exchange surfaces like lungs. Without them, oxygen couldn't diffuse fast enough to the centre of the body.

B–A*

Breathing

Ventilation

- Ventilation is moving air into and out of the lungs.
- Air that is breathed in is called inspired air, air that is breathed out is called expired air.
- The lungs don't have muscles, so air is pushed and pulled by muscles in-between the ribs and the diaphragm.

Figure 3: Breathing in (inspiration)

Figure 4: Breathing out (expiration)

rib   trachea   lung

backbone   one set of intercostal muscles contracts   diaphragm muscles contracted

- movement of air
- movement of ribs
- movement of diaphragm

rib muscles relaxed

diaphragm muscles relaxed

D–C

Control of breathing

- Breathing is mostly controlled unconsciously but you can affect your breathing rate, e.g. holding your breath under water.
- Your breathing rate increases when more oxygen is needed for respiration, e.g. when doing exercise.
- Breathing faster increases the amount of oxygen in the blood.
- The brain detects the amount of carbon dioxide in the blood, produced by respiration.
- Signals pass along nerves from the brain to the muscles to contract and relax more frequently.

B–A*

Improve your grade

For each gas, explain the difference between the inspired and expired air. AO2 (2 marks)

more oxygen, less CO₂, air is water vapour is ~~~ for respiration

	inspired air	expired air
nitrogen	79%	79%
oxygen	20.97%	16.9%
carbon dioxide	0.03%	4.1%
water vapour	variable	saturated

What do plants need?

- Plants need light, carbon dioxide and water to photosynthesise.
  - To absorb light, they have large flat leaves.
  - To absorb carbon dioxide, they have pores on the underside of the leaf called stomata.
  - The leaves are thin, so that the gases can diffuse to the cells in the middle of the leaf.
  - To absorb water, root hair cells have an extension to increase their surface area for osmosis.

- Plants also need minerals, which are absorbed by the root by diffusion or active transport.

D–C

Cells in the leaf

- There are two arrangements of cells in the leaf.
  - At the top of the leaf, they are fitted closely together to trap all of the light.
  - In the middle of the leaf, there are gaps between cells to allow gases to diffuse in and out of the cells.

B–A*

Remember!
Plants make food from photosynthesis, they then use the food to release energy in respiration.

Transpiration

Movement of water in plants

- Transpiration is the diffusion of water from the stomata.

- Water moves from inside of the cell, across the membranes, then evaporates from the cell walls.

- Water vapour then moves through the spaces to the stomata.

- Stomata have guard cells, which can open and close to regulate the rate of transpiration.

D–C

When the guard cells have plenty of water, they bend apart and open the stoma.

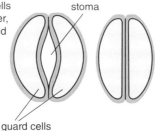

stoma

When the guard cells do not have much water, they become less curved and close the stoma.

guard cells

Figure 1: How stomata can be opened and closed

- If the plant is at risk of wilting (when the cells don't have enough water), the guard cells close the stoma.

Changing rates of transpiration

- As water diffuses out of the stomata, it draws water and minerals into the roots.
- High temperature increases the rate of transpiration because the water molecules have more kinetic energy.
- Wind increases the rate of transpiration by taking away the water that surrounds the leaf and increasing the concentration gradient.
- Dry weather increases the rate of transpiration because of the increase in the concentration gradient.
- Transpiration can act as a coolant which stops the plant burning on hot days.
- Plants that live in hot, dry places may only open their stomata at night to limit water loss.

B–A*

Improve your grade

Sasha looked at the stomata in two ivy plants, she found that the plant that grew in full sunlight had less stomata. Suggest a reason for this. **AO2 (2 marks)**

rate of Transpiration higher, less stomata needed.

The circulatory system

The structure of the heart

- The circulatory system transports molecules around the body.
- It is made up of the heart and blood vessels.
- Oxygen is transported to cells for use in respiration.
- Carbon dioxide is transported to the lungs after it is made in respiration.
- Nutrients are transported from the digestive system to cells.
- The heart is made of muscle tissue, by contracting and relaxing it pushes the blood around the body.
- There are four chambers in total: the atria (top two chambers) receive blood; the ventricles (bottom two chambers) pump blood.
- Blood in the left carries lots of oxygen, whereas blood in the right has very little oxygen.
- To keep blood going in the right direction, valves open and close in the large arteries; between the atria; and between the atria and the ventricles.

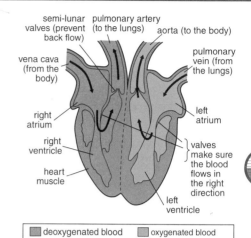

Figure 2: Inside the human heart (the heart is shown as if the person was facing you)

D–C

EXAM TIP

In diagrams, the left-hand side of the heart is bigger.

Sides of the heart

- Blood leaves the left side of the heart via the aorta, travels round the body then returns to the right side of the heart via the vena cava.
- Blood travels to the lungs in the pulmonary artery, the only artery to carry deoxygenated blood; and returns to the heart in the pulmonary vein, the only vein to carry oxygenated blood.

B–A*

Blood vessels

Types of vessels

- Arteries carry blood away from the heart.
- Arteries carry blood under high pressure, so they have thick and elastic walls so they can stretch.
- Coronary arteries deliver blood to the heart.
- Capillaries carry blood to cells and are needed for transport.
- Capillaries are one cell thick for easy diffusion.
- Veins carry blood back to the heart.
- Veins carry blood under lower pressure so they have valves to prevent the backflow of blood.

artery – thick walls containing muscle and elastic fibres

vein – thinner walls, containing some muscle and elastic fibres, also have valves

capillary – tiny, with walls only one cell thick

Figure 3: The three types of blood vessels

D–C

Cholesterol and the heart

- Cholesterol can build up in blood vessels, forming plaques.
- If a plaque blocks a coronary artery, it can lead to a heart attack.
- A little tube called a stent can be inserted into the coronary artery to keep it open.

B–A*

Improve your grade

Explain how the structure of an artery is related to its function. **AO1 (4 marks)**

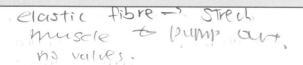

elastic fibre → strech
muscle to pump out
no valves.

Blood

Composition of the blood

D–C

- Most of the blood is a pale yellow liquid called plasma.

- Plasma carries dissolved nutrients, like glucose and amino acids; and waste, like urea and carbon dioxide.

- Red blood cells contain haemoglobin, which carries oxygen.

- When haemoglobin binds to oxygen it becomes oxyhaemoglobin, which is bright red.

- Oxygenated blood is carrying oxygen; blood without oxygen is deoxygenated and is a duller colour.

- White blood cells defend the body against microorganisms.

- Platelets are needed for blood clotting.

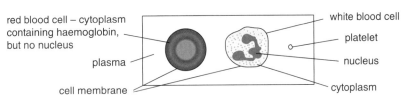

red blood cell – cytoplasm containing haemoglobin, but no nucleus

plasma

cell membrane

white blood cell

platelet

nucleus

cytoplasm

Figure 1: The components of blood

Changes in the blood

B–A*

- When blood passes through the lungs, carbon dioxide diffuses out and oxygen diffuses in.

- When blood passes through the small intestine, it absorbs nutrients.

- When blood passes through the kidneys, urea diffuses out.

- Blood is classed as a tissue because it is a group of cells with a similar structure and function.

Transport in plants

Xylem and phloem

D–C

- In plants, the transport system is made of cells joined together.

- Xylem tissue transports water and dissolved minerals from the roots to the stem and the leaves.

- Xylem tissue is made out of the remains of dead cells and is hollow.

- Phloem tissue transports dissolved sugars from the leaves to other parts of the plant.

- Water moves through the plant by transpiration.

- The loss of water through the leaves reduces the pressure in the xylem.

- Water flows from the high pressure in the roots to the lower pressure in the stem.

- The movement of water from roots to leaves is the transpiration stream.

- Transpiration can be measured using a photometer.

- Hotter, dryer and windier conditions increase the rate of transpiration.

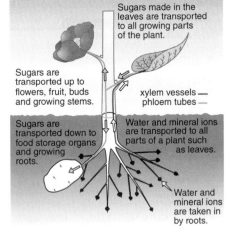

Sugars made in the leaves are transported to all growing parts of the plant.

Sugars are transported up to flowers, fruit, buds and growing stems.

xylem vessels — phloem tubes —

Sugars are transported down to food storage organs and growing roots.

Water and mineral ions are transported to all parts of a plant such as leaves.

Water and mineral ions are taken in by roots.

Figure 2: The two transport systems in a plant

EXAM TIP

Remember 'xy' goes up high and 'phlo' goes down low.

Water movement through the plant

B–A*

- Water enters the root-hair cells by osmosis and then must move through the root till it reaches the xylem.

Improve your grade

Describe the transport system in plants. **AO1 (2 marks)**

Waste and water control

Types of waste

- Waste products must be removed from the body.
- Carbon dioxide is a waste product from respiration in all body cells.
- Carbon dioxide is removed by the lungs.
- Urea is a waste product made from excess amino acids in the liver.
- Urea is removed by the kidneys.
- Urea is transported in the blood to the kidneys.
- Kidneys filter the blood, absorbing everything except cells and large molecules.
- Useful nutrients like glucose are reabsorbed, leaving urea and excess water and ions.
- The urea, water and minerals form urine, which is stored in the bladder until urination.

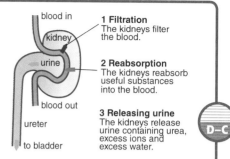

1 Filtration
The kidneys filter the blood.

2 Reabsorption
The kidneys reabsorb useful substances into the blood.

3 Releasing urine
The kidneys release urine containing urea, excess ions and excess water.

Figure 3: How kidneys make urine

D–C

Homeostasis

- Keeping the levels of the body constant, like its water and temperature, is called homeostasis.

B–A*

Treating kidney disease

Transplants and dialysis

- Kidney failure can be treated by dialysis or a kidney transplant.
- A kidney transplant can be from a healthy donor, or someone who has recently died.
- An advantage of transplants is that if it works the recipient can lead a normal life.
- Disadvantages of transplants include the risk of rejection by the recipient's body and the lack of available kidneys.
- A dialysis machine acts like a substitute kidney.
- Blood flows into the machine and waste substances are removed along with excess water.
- Dialysis fluid has the correct concentration of essential substances like glucose, and no urea, so urea diffuses into the fluid and glucose stays in the blood.
- Dialysis is useful because it is more widely available than transplants and there is no risk of rejection.
- Disadvantages of dialysis: it takes several hours and must be done more than once a week, patients are more likely to fall ill and it does not cure the problem.

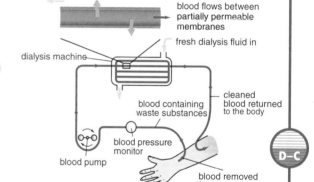

urea diffuses out of the blood into the dialysis fluid

blood flows between partially permeable membranes

fresh dialysis fluid in

dialysis machine

cleaned blood returned to the body

blood containing waste substances

blood pressure monitor

blood pump

blood removed from a vein

Figure 4: How dialysis works

D–C

Problems with dialysis

- A recipient's body can attack the donor kidney because it has foreign antigens and the body treats it like harmful bacteria.
- To stop rejection, donor kidneys are matched to the recipient to ensure they have a similar tissue type.
- Recipients have to take immunosuppressant drugs for the rest of their lives to stop their immune system attacking the donor kidney.

B–A*

Improve your grade

Describe how kidneys help get rid of the body's waste products. AO1 (4 marks)

substance in blood diffuse to through PPM in kidney, and th
but uretus, body reabsorb all glucose, and correct amm
of Water & th content. excess pass with urea to form urine stored

Temperature control

Effects of temperature on the body

D–C

- Mammals and birds can control their body temperature.
- In humans, if body temperatures go too high or too low we feel sick and can even die.
- The thermoregulatory centre in the brain controls the body temperature.
- Temperature sensors on the skin send messages to the brain and so can make you feel hot or cold.
- The core body temperature mostly stays at 37 °C.
- When we are too hot, skin arterioles dilate, more blood goes to the skin's surface and energy is lost by radiation.
- When we are too hot, sweat glands secrete sweat, the sweat evaporates using heat energy from the skin and so cools us down.
- When we are too cold, skin arterioles contract and blood is kept away from the skin.
- When we are too cold, muscles contract rapidly, making us shiver, generating heat from the respiration needed to fuel the muscles.

Effects of temperature on cells

B–A*

- A constant body temperature is needed for efficient chemical reactions in our cells.
- If body temperature drops, chemical reactions happen much slower.
- If body temperature rises, enzymes can denature and this can stop the reactions.

Controlling blood glucose

Glucose levels and diabetes

D–C

- Glucose is needed to fuel respiration, it is carried to cells in the blood.
- If blood glucose levels drop too low, the brain cells are affected and the person may faint.
- If blood glucose levels are too high, water is drawn out of the cells by osmosis and can cause permanent harm.
- The pancreas detects blood glucose levels and secretes insulin when it gets too high.
- People who don't secrete insulin have type I diabetes which cannot be cured.
- People with type I diabetes have to:
  - eat little amounts and often so their blood glucose levels don't rise too much
  - inject insulin before meals
  - be more careful with exercise by either eating more, or injecting less insulin.

Glucose levels and hormones

B–A*

- Insulin makes cells take in glucose from the blood.
- Liver cells store the glucose as an insoluble molecule called glycogen.
- If blood glucose levels drop too low, the pancreas releases glucagon.
- Glucagon causes the liver to break down glycogen into glucose and release it into the blood.

> **Remember!**
> GlucagON is a hormONe, glycogen is a carbohydrate.

Improve your grade

You come across someone who is shaking and looking pale, suggest what might be wrong with them with reasons.
AO2 (3 marks) too cold, muscle contract, respiration release heat energy to keep it warmer, arteries contract, blood is away from skin, less blood flow through. less heat lost.

Human waste

Effects of human population growth

- Rapid human population growth combined with an increase in living standard means there is more waste produced.

- Water can be polluted by sewage, fertilisers and toxic chemicals:
  - sewage lowers the oxygen concentration killing aquatic animals.

- Air can be polluted by smoke and by gases such as sulfur dioxide:
  - smoke produced by burning fossil fuels can lead to asthma and respiratory illnesses
  - sulfur dioxide from burning fossil fuels contributes to acid rain, which kills animals.

- Land can be polluted by pesticides and herbicides:
  - pesticides used in farming can kill animals that are not pests
  - herbicides used in farming can kill plants that are not weeds and may harm animals.

- There is less land for wildlife because it is used in:
  - building houses, schools and hospitals
  - quarrying to obtain materials from under the ground
  - farming to produce food.

Making difficult decisions

- Making decisions about what should be done is difficult because the problems caused must be compared against the progress made. For example:
  - the M6 toll road made journeys quicker and reduced pollution from cars in traffics jams
  - the M6 toll road also used up land that could be used for wildlife and may encourage more people to drive rather than use public transport.

Deforestation

The effects of deforestation

- Deforestation occurs when trees are harvested unsustainably.

- Unsustainable harvesting includes slash and burn, when trees are cut down and their roots burnt.

- Deforestation has occurred so that crops can be planted to use for food, biofuels or for livestock, and to harvest timber.
  ↑ biofuel , ethanol
- Cattle and rice paddies both increase the levels of methane in the atmosphere.

- Deforestation leads to a decrease in biodiversity because wildlife loses a habitat.

- Deforestation leads to an increase in greenhouse gases because the carbon locked in trees is released by burning, and it reduces the capture of carbon dioxide by photosynthesis.

- Peat bogs have also been harvested unsustainably for fuel and to improve the water-holding of soil. Peat bogs contain partly rotted vegetation, which traps carbon dioxide. If the peat bogs are destroyed, the carbon dioxide is released.

> **EXAM TIP**
>
> Don't forget to link deforestation to increased greenhouse gases.

Peat bogs and bacteria

- Vegetation doesn't rot in peat bogs because there are low oxygen levels due to the amount of water.

- If there isn't enough oxygen, bacteria can't break down the vegetation.

- If the peat bog dries out, the bacteria can break down the vegetation releasing the stored carbon as carbon dioxide produced by respiration.

⊙ Improve your grade

Explain the reasons for deforestation. **AO1 (3 marks)**

Global temperature

Increasing global temperature

- The mean global temperature is increasing, this is global warming.

- This happens naturally but scientists think that human activity is affecting the increase.

- Even small changes in temperature can have many effects, the impacts may be:
  - changes in climate – drought in some places, floods in others
  - a rise in sea level – water expands when heated and ice caps are melting, coastal areas will be most affected
  - a reduction in biodiversity – some species may not be able to adapt and may become extinct
  - changes in species distribution – some species may migrate to other places to escape the changing climate
  - changes in migration patterns – birds which normally migrate south for the winter may stop migrating.

- Slowing the rise of carbon dioxide levels can occur through an increase in natural storage, like peat bogs and forests.

- Oceans can store carbon dioxide through sequestration: algae absorb carbon dioxide through photosynthesis and shellfish use carbon to make their shells, when they die they sink to the bottom taking the carbon with them.

- Biofuels, made from the fermentation of plant products, could replace fossil fuels.

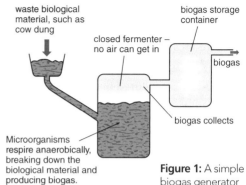

Figure 1: A simple biogas generator

waste biological material, such as cow dung

closed fermenter – no air can get in

biogas storage container

biogas

biogas collects

Microorganisms respire anaerobically, breaking down the biological material and producing biogas.

D–C

Biofuels

B–A*

- Biofuels include biogas (a mixture of methane and other gases), bioethanol (produced by yeast fermentation), and biodiesel (made from plant oils).

- Predicting what will happen with climate change is difficult because the processes are complex and future emissions cannot be predicted.

Food production

Farming and food miles

D–C

- At each stage in a food chain only 10% of the energy is passed from one stage to the next.

- The lower the position in the food chain, the more efficient the food production.

- Energy can be conserved by reducing available movement for livestock by keeping them in small pens.

- Keeping animals warm will also reduce energy loss through respiration.

- If food comes from nearby it is more energy efficient than imported food, the distance food travels is called food miles.

- The greater the food miles, the more greenhouse emissions there are from transport.

Being vegetarian

B–A*

- In developing countries being vegetarian may not be an option because:
  - the soil is too dry to grow crops
  - there may be a limited number of possible crops that can be grown
  - people may need the essential proteins and vitamins found in meat
  - animals can survive through a winter that plants can't.

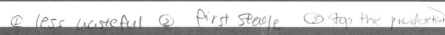
① less wasteful ② first stage ③ top the production of nothing

◉ Improve your grade

Explain why it is better for the environment to be a vegetarian. **AO2 (3 marks)**

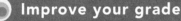
no energy lost since it is the first stage, less food miles.

Harvesting fish

Unsustainable fishing

- When fish are taken from the sea faster than they can breed it is unsustainable.

- Unsustainable fishing leads to smaller fish, low fish stocks and extinction.

- Fisherman don't want to reduce their catches because they need to make a living.

- Trying to fish sustainably is called managing fish stocks and this can be done by:
  - banning nets with small holes, so smaller fish can escape
  - imposing quotas, so that a limited amount of fish can be caught
  - individuals only buying sustainably caught fish.

- Fish farming is not sustainable because many smaller fish are needed to feed one large fish like a tuna.

International fishing

- In order to impose quotas, there needs to be international cooperation.

- Europe has imposed quotas and has shared them out between countries.

Fungus and mycoprotein

Making mycoprotein

- Mycoprotein is a protein-rich alternative to meat and fish.

- Mycoprotein can be shaped and flavoured to look like food.

- Mycoprotein is high in protein and fibre and low in fat, making it a healthy food.

- *Fusarium* is a fungus grown in large vats and then turned into mycoprotein.

- Glucose that is obtained from waste from other processes is used to feed *Fusarium*.

- The fermenter is adjusted to make the ideal conditions for maximum growth rate.

- The contents cannot be stirred because it would disrupt the hyphae which make up the fungus.

- Air is bubbled through the mixture to supply oxygen for aerobic respiration and to mix up the contents.

- The fungus is harvested and purified before sale.

Remember!

An example of mycoprotein is Quorn.®

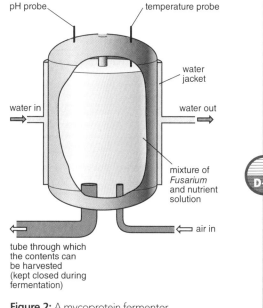

Figure 2: A mycoprotein fermenter

(labels: pH probe, temperature probe, water jacket, water in, water out, mixture of *Fusarium* and nutrient solution, air in, tube through which the contents can be harvested (kept closed during fermentation))

Efficiency and mycoprotein

- The hyphae give the food a texture similar to meat.

- Because *Fusarium* is one of the first stages of the food chain, ecologically it is a more efficient way of eating protein than meat as there is more energy available.

Improve your grade

Give one ecological, one ethical and one health reason why it is better to eat mycoprotein than meat.
AO1 and 2 (3 marks)

First in food, don't kill ... high in protein & fibre, low in fat

B3 Summary

Osmosis is the movement of water from a dilute concentration to a concentrated solution.

Entering cells

Osmosis needs a partially permeable membrane.

Active transport requires energy.

Diffusion and osmosis are passive, so they happen without energy.

Water enters root hair cells by osmosis.

Animal cells burst in a dilute concentration because too much water enters by osmosis.

Alveoli are needed to get oxygen into the blood and carbon dioxide out of the blood.

Active transport goes against the concentration gradient.

Cells shrink if they are placed into a concentrated solution because water leaves by osmosis.

Plant cells don't burst in a dilute concentration because of the cell wall.

Exchange surfaces are adapted for efficient diffusion.

Ventilation exchanges gases in the lungs.

Getting around

The heart pumps blood around the body.

Blood carries oxygen and nutrients to cells and carries away carbon dioxide and urea.

Xylem carries water and minerals from the roots to the leaves of the plant.

Phloem carries dissolved sugar in the plant.

Arteries carry blood away from the heart and veins carry blood to the heart.

The movement of water around the plant is called transpiration.

The diaphragm and rib muscles are needed for ventilation.

Kidneys remove urea and excess water from the blood.

Balancing the body

Body temperature is controlled by the contraction of skin arterioles, sweating and shivering.

Dialysis and kidney transplants are treatments for kidney failure.

In diabetes, the pancreas can't make insulin.

Blood glucose is controlled by hormones released by the pancreas.

Dialysis take up a lot of time because it needs to be done every day.

Kidney transplants can mean that a person can lead a normal life.

Kidney transplants may be rejected.

Deforestation results in increased greenhouse gases and loss of biodiversity.

Sustainability

Farmers keep animals warm and stop them from moving to save energy.

Biofuels could replace fossil fuels.

Food brought from further away has more food miles.

Deforestation occurs to have more land for agriculture and building.

Overfishing may lead to smaller fish, low fish stocks or extinction.

Eating from lower down the food chain is more efficient.

Human waste is increasing because of increased living standards and population growth.

International cooperation is needed to stop overfishing.

Mycoprotein is made from fungus and is high in protein and low in fat.

Improve your grade

B1 Improve your grade

Page 6

Harry's diet is very high in saturated fats. Suggest two ways that this could affect his health. **AO2 (3 marks)**

It will make him put on weight.

This answer got 1 mark out of 3 (grade EF). To improve the answer, the candidate should have stated another way that Harry's diet could affect his health. A diet high in saturated fat will increase the risk of developing heart disease. Also, it is scientifically correct to use the term 'mass' instead of weight in this case.

Page 7

Use the graph to explain the change in the number of pathogens. **AO2 (4 marks)**

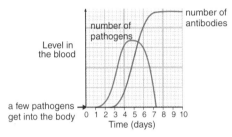

The number of pathogens started to increase, then after 5 days they started to decrease. This happened because the number of antibodies had increased which started to destroy the pathogens.

This answer got 3 marks out of 4 (grade B). The candidate described the rise in the number of pathogens but did not explain why this happened (the pathogens would start to reproduce). Including the time when the numbers of pathogens went down was good.

Page 8

Explain why a doctor will not prescribe you antibiotics for a bacterial throat infection. **AO2 (3 marks)**

Because we need to stop using so many antibiotics.

This answer achieved 1 mark out of a possible 3 (grade C/D), as it stated a fact but did not go on to explain why doctors should not prescribe antibiotics for this infection. A simple throat infection, although uncomfortable, will soon be cleared up by the person's own white blood cells. Using antibiotics gives an advantage to any antibiotic-resistant bacteria that may have formed in the throat by only killing off the non-resistant bacteria and allowing the resistant ones to reproduce.

Page 9

You wish to grow some harmless E. coli bacteria on some agar jelly. You use an inoculating loop to transfer the bacteria to the jelly. Explain why it is important to hold the inoculating loop in a flame first.
AO1 (2 marks)

To make it sterile.

This answer gets 1 of the marks (grade D) as the candidate forgot to mention why making the loop sterile is important. It is to prevent the agar becoming contaminated with any other type of microorganism.

Page 10

An injury that results in breaking of the spine may result in the person being paralysed. Explain why.
AO2 (3 marks)

The nerves in the spine might be broken.

This answer only makes one suggestion and thus only achieves one of the three possible marks (grade E/F). To gain full marks, explain that the spinal cord is part of the central nervous system and contains many neurones that send messages from the brain to all parts of the body. When these impulses meet the muscles, they contract. If the nerves in the spinal cord are broken then impulses cannot cross them, so muscles will not respond.

Page 11

James is dancing in a nightclub. He starts to sweat. Explain how sweating helps to cool him down.
AO2 (2 marks)

The sweat evaporates from his skin. It needs energy to change from a liquid into a gas and so uses the heat from the skin as a source of the energy. This cools down the skin and reduces his body temperature.

This answer gets full marks and so achieves an A* grade. The candidate has shown that they have a deep understanding of the science by adding the information about why the skin needs heat to evaporate.

Page 12

FSH is found in fertility drugs. Explain how taking FSH will increase a woman's fertility. **AO2 (2 marks)**

It will increase the amount of eggs that mature in her ovaries.

This answer achieves one of the two possible marks (grade D). The candidate should have continued to explain that increasing the amount of mature eggs means that more than one will be released at a time, which will increase the chance of one being fertilised.

Page 13

Explain how the hormone auxin brings about a response to light called phototropism. **AO2 (4 marks)**

Light shines on the plant from one direction. There is more auxin on the shaded side so there are more cells here. This bends the shoot towards the light.

This answer gets two marks (grade D). The candidate has misunderstood how auxins affect plant growth. They do not increase the number of cells but increase the length of them.

Page 14

Some doctors believe that everyone over the age of 50 should be prescribed statins on the NHS for free. Evaluate this decision. **AO2 (4 marks)**

It is a good decision because trials have shown that statins reduce blood cholesterol levels, so it will reduce their risk of dying from a heart attack.

The candidate has achieved two marks out of a possible four (grade C). For a higher grade, they need to give any disadvantages of this decision. For example, some people over 50 do not have high cholesterol so do not need statins. For them, they would be taking a drug that they do not need which could waste the NHS's money. Also, there is now evidence that statins have side-effects.

Page 15

Explain how cacti are adapted to living in the dry desert. **AO2 (3 marks)**

Cacti have long roots to grow deep into the soil and spread out as well as to absorb maximum amounts of water. They can also store water in its tissues to use when they can't absorb any water from the ground. They have no leaves, which reduces water lost by evaporation. Their spikes stop animals from eating them.

This answer gets full marks (grade A). The candidate has described all of its features and explained how they enable the cactus to have a supply of water at all times, which is the main problem for a plant living in the desert. They have shown extra knowledge by explaining the function of the spikes.*

Page 16

Sewage contains a lot of microorganisms. Explain why mayfly larva cannot live in water polluted with sewage. **AO2 (2 marks)**

The microorganisms are pathogens and kill the mayfly larva.

The candidate has not achieved any marks for this question (grade U), as they have not understood how microorganisms will kill the larva. Increasing the amount of microorganisms in the water will decrease the amount of dissolved oxygen. The oxygen-loving mayfly larvae would not be able to survive in water with low levels of dissolved oxygen.

Page 17

Explain why biomass decreases as you move along a food chain. **AO2 (3 marks)**

The amount of energy decreases as you go along a food chain. Less energy means less biomass.

This answer gets two marks (grade B). The candidate should have gone on to explain why the energy decreases. A suitable reason might be that energy is wasted as heat, and in waste such as urine.

Page 18

Write a simple plan for an investigation to prove that the decay of bread by mould requires moisture. **AO2 (2 marks)**

Take 2 slices of bread. Add a little water to one. Place both in a plastic bag and leave in a warm place.

This answer has achieved 3 marks out of 4 (grade C). The candidate has not explained how they would compare the decay of each one. They could just look at the growth of mould on each slice. An even better method is to measure the area of each slice that is covered with mould.

Page 19

Emma and Alice are identical twins. Emma has blonde hair and Alice has brown hair. Is this variation due to genetics or the environment? Explain your answer. **AO2 (2 marks)**

It is due to the environment because they are identical twins so have the same genes.

This answer gets full marks (grade A). To further show knowledge, the candidate could have explained why they have the same genes: identical twins are formed when a fertilised egg splits in half.

Page 20

Buttercup the cow produces the most milk in her herd. Her farmer is considering using her eggs for embryo transplants. Explain to him why cloning her might be an even better idea. **AO2 (3 marks)**

If you clone her then you will get another cow exactly like her who will produce lots of milk.

This answer gained two marks out of three (grade B). To get full marks, the answer should explain why in this case cloning is better than embryo transplants. Embryo transplants involve using the eggs from the animal with desired characteristics and fertilising them with sperm from a male animal. The resulting embryos will have a mix of genes from both parents, and not necessarily the desired ones that you were trying to achieve. Cloning animals will produce offspring that are identical to the parent.

Page 21

In 1859, Charles Darwin published a book containing his ideas about natural selection and evolution. Explain why many people at the time did not believe what it said. **AO2 (3 marks)**

Most people thought that God had created all the living things on Earth in the form that they are in now.

The candidate correctly identified one of the reasons why people did not accept Darwin's theory, so achieves one mark out of three (grade D). They should also have explained that nobody understood how characteristics of the parent could be passed to its offspring, as genes had not yet been discovered. Also, at that time, there was not much scientific evidence to support the theory.

Page 22

The cheetah is the fastest land animal on Earth. It uses its speed to catch its prey. Use natural selection to explain how cheetahs have got faster over time.
AO2 (5 marks)

The cheetahs that were the quickest caught prey and survived.

This answer gained two marks out of five (grade E/D). The candidate should have put much more information into their answer. When tackling questions about natural selection, apply these stages: Some cheetahs were faster than others (variation). The fastest cheetahs caught more prey than the slower ones (competition). They survived (survival) to reproduce and pass on the genes for speed onto their offspring (reproduction). If this keeps happening, then over many generations the cheetah will get faster.

B2 Improve your grade

Page 24

The image below was taken of some cells using a light microscope. State what type of cells they are and give reasons for your answer. **AO2 (2 marks)**

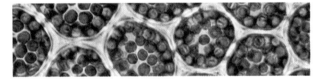

Plant cells because they are green.

This answer gains 1 mark out of 2 (grade B). The candidate identified the correct type of cell but the reason given was not sufficient. To gain full marks the answer should have talked about organelles: it could have mentioned that these cells contain chloroplasts or that they have a cell wall. Full marks would also be given if the candidate said they were algae cells.

Page 25

Explain how a sperm cell is specialised. **AO2 (4 marks)**

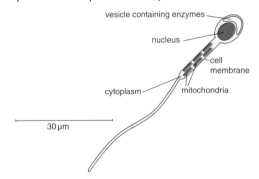

It has a tail to help it swim.

This answer gains 1 mark out of 4 (grade D). The candidate correctly identified that it has a tail for swimming but did not explain why this is required (to reach the egg for fertilisation). To gain full marks, the answer needs to include at least two of the adaptations explained. For example, the candidate could have

mentioned that the sperm has a vesicle containing enzymes, which are used to digest the outside of the egg to allow the nucleus of the sperm to fuse with the nucleus of the egg during fertilisation.

Page 26

Describe why the stomach is classed as an organ.
AO2 (2 marks)

It contains lots of cells.

This answer did not achieve any marks (grade U), as the candidate did not understand what we mean by an organ. To gain full marks the answer should explain that the stomach is an organ because it is made up of lots of different tissues, which work together to carry out a function.
(It would not be necessary, although interesting, to write that the tissues are glandular tissue to secretes juices, muscular tissue to contract the stomach walls, and epithelial tissue to protect the stomach from the juices it makes.)

Page 27

Without photosynthesis, humans would not survive. Explain why. **AO2 (2 marks)**

Photosynthesis produces oxygen which we need to live.

This answer gains 1 mark out of 2 (grade B). To achieve maximum marks, the candidate should have also explained that photosynthesis produces glucose, which is a store of energy. Animals eat the plant and release the energy which is also essential for life.

Page 28

Anna uses a fertiliser that is high in nitrates on her tomato plants. Explain why she does this. **AO2 (3 marks)**

So the plants have nitrates which they can use to make protein.

This answer gains 2 marks out of a possible 3 (grade B). To achieve the missing mark, the candidate should have gone on to explain why proteins are essential for the healthy growth of the plant: they are used to build new cells. (It would not be necessary, although interesting, to write that the proteins are also used to build enzymes. Also, that without a supply of nitrate, the tomato plants would not grow to their full potential nor produce many tomatoes. Plants absorb minerals such as nitrates through their roots, so this is why fertilisers are added to the soil.)

Page 29

Simon went on holiday to Mexico. He noticed that the plants growing there were very different to the plants growing at home in the UK. Explain the reasons for this difference in distribution. **AO2 (3 marks)**

The temperature is much warmer in Mexico, so the plants that grow there are adapted to living at higher temperatures. The rainfall is also lower in Mexico, so the plants there have adaptations to help them cope with lack of water.

This answer gains full marks (grade A) as the candidate mentioned two differences in physical factors between Mexico and the UK, and explained how these affect the distribution of the plants. The plants growing in Mexico may not survive in the UK because of the low temperatures and high rainfall.

Page 30

Pepsin is an enzyme that helps break down proteins in the stomach. It has an optimum pH of 2. Use this information to explain why the stomach produces hydrochloric acid. **AO2 (2 marks)**

Pepsin has an optimum pH of 2 so it works best in acidic conditions.

This answer gained 1 mark out of a possible 2 (grade B). The answer did not really explain what is meant by optimum pH and why this is important. The optimum pH is the pH at which an enzyme works best at. The acid produced by the stomach means that pepsin can break down protein in the stomach at a fast rate.

Page 31

Dipesh mixed some starch with amylase in a beaker and left the mixture in a water bath at 37 °C. After 30 minutes, he tested the mixture to see if there was any starch present. Predict what he will find and give a reason for your answer. **AO2 (2 marks)**

There would be no starch left because the amylase breaks down starch.

This answer achieves full marks (grade A) but it would be more complete, and show the candidate's knowledge better, if it included the fact that the starch would have been broken down into sugars. Remember that enzymes are only catalysts in the breaking down of food. The starch would eventually break down by itself, it would just take a lot longer.

Page 32

Explain why breathing rate increases when you exercise. **AO2 (3 marks)**

Your muscles are contracting quickly so are using up energy at a fast rate. Breathing rate increases to get oxygen to the muscles quickly.

This answer gains 2 marks out of a possible 3 (grade B). For full marks, the candidate needs to go on to explain why the muscles need a good supply of oxygen: to carry out aerobic respiration in order to release energy from glucose. The energy is used to enable the muscles to contract. If you are aiming for an A* grade it is a good idea to include word equations wherever possible: glucose + oxygen → carbon dioxide + water (+ energy).

Page 33

You are involved in a race. At first you sprint off feeling full of energy. However, halfway through, your legs start to ache and you have to stop. Explain why this happened. **AO2 (3 marks)**

My heart could not beat fast enough and my lungs could not breathe fast enough to get oxygen to my leg muscles, so they could not carry out respiration and make energy for my leg muscles to work.

This answer gains 1 mark (grade C/D). The candidate was correct in stating that the lungs and heart could not work fast enough to get the required levels of oxygen to the leg muscles but respiration would not stop – anaerobic respiration would take over. For full marks, the answer should explain this, then go on to explain that the legs would start to ache and stop working efficiently because of the build-up of lactic acid in the muscle cells.

Page 34

Explain why mitosis is an essential process in the formation of a baby from a fertilised egg. **AO2 (2 marks)**

Mitosis is needed to produce the egg and sperm cells that join to form the fertilised egg.

This answer is incorrect and will score no marks (grade U). The candidate has mixed up the terms mitosis and meiosis. For full marks the answer should state that the fertilised egg is one cell (called a zygote), which will divide by mitosis to form the many cells that make up a baby.

Page 35

In the future, we may be able to use an individual's genome to calculate the likelihood of them developing certain diseases such as cancer. Evaluate this potential application. **AO2 (6 marks)**

If a person's DNA shows they might get a disease, they might not be able to get a job because the employer is worried about them getting ill and taking time off work. But it might be useful to know this, as you can be told about what symptoms to look out for and how to change your lifestyle to reduce the risk of the illness developing. However, you are not told if you will definitely develop the disease, only if you are more slightly at risk. This might cause people to worry and some people would rather not know.

The candidate has fully evaluated this new technology by giving detailed benefits and drawbacks (grade A).

Page 36

Katy has red hair. Both her parents have brown hair. Explain how Katy inherited red hair when her parents do not have it. **AO2 (3 marks)**

Katy got the gene for red hair from her parents.

This answer gains 1 mark out of 3 (grade D). To achieve full marks, the candidate needs to explain why Katy's parents do not have red hair. The red-hair allele must be recessive. Her parents both have the red-hair allele but their other allele (brown hair) masks it. Katy received two red-hair alleles from her parents during fertilisation so Katy has two red-hair alleles (her genotype) and so therefore has red hair (her phenotype). Also, to show a good understanding of genetics, the candidate should have used the correct terminology. Red hair should be referred to as an allele, not a gene. The red hair allele is a type of hair-colour gene.

Page 37

The height of pea plants is controlled by a single gene. The tall allele is dominant. A tall pea plant was bred with a short pea plant. The offspring formed was in the ratio 1 tall : 1 short. Draw a genetic diagram to show the cross. **AO2 (4 marks)**

Parents	tall pea plant	short pea plant
	TT	tt
Gametes	T and T	t and t

Offspring		T	T
	t	Tt	Tt
	t	Tt	Tt

This answer gains 2 marks out of 4 (grade C). The candidate has made a mistake in determining the allele of the tall pea plant. You can see from the cross that all of the offspring are tall, not the ratio of 1 tall : 1 short. The tall plant must have the alleles Tt.

Page 38

Polydactyly is caused by a dominant allele. Jessica has polydactyly. Ryan does not have it. Could their children have polydactyly? Explain your answer. **AO2 (3 marks)**

Yes, because they could inherit the polydactyly gene from Jessica.

This answer gains 2 marks (grade B). To gain full marks, the candidate should go on to explain that the children only need one dominant allele in order to have polydactyly and, as Jessica has the disorder, she must carry at least one dominant allele.

Page 39

Around 300 years ago, the dodo lived on the island of Mauritius. It had no predators. People arrived on the island. They brought predators such as dogs, pigs and rats. Explain why the dodo became extinct. **AO2 (2 marks)**

The dodos got eaten by the dogs, pigs and rats and they all died out.

This answer gains 1 mark out of 2 (grade B). To achieve full marks, the candidate should have added that the dodo was not adapted to escape the new predators and was not able to evolve quickly enough.

B3 Improve your grade

Page 41

Iodine turns starch a blue-black colour. The diagram shows what happens when starch is put into visking tubing and placed into a beaker of water containing iodine. Explain why the water remains brown but inside the visking tubing it is blue-black. **AO2 and 3 (2 marks)**

The starch is too big to get out of the visking tubing. But the water is small enough to move in. So the starch turns blue-black.

This answer gains 1 mark (grade D/C). The candidate's first sentence is correct, the second sentence is also true, however it is the movement of iodine which turns the starch blue-black not the movement of water, so the second mark is lost.

Page 42

If people with Coeliac disease eat wheat, their villi can be damaged and become flattened. How and why would this effect the absorption of nutrients? **AO2 (2 marks)**

The flattened villi couldn't absorb as many nutrients.

This answer gains 1 mark (grade D/C). The sentence is correct so gets one mark. To gain full marks the candidate needs to explain why – it is because the flattened villi have a smaller surface area. Always make sure you add enough points for each mark.

Page 43

For each gas, explain the difference between the inspired and expired air. **AO2 (2 marks)**

	inspired air	expired air
nitrogen	79%	79%
oxygen	20.97%	16.9%
carbon dioxide	0.03%	4.1%
water vapour	variable	saturated

Nitrogen isn't absorbed, oxygen is used in respiration, carbon dioxide is breathed out and water comes from spit.

This answer gains 2 marks (grade D/C). The candidate's first two explanations for nitrogen and oxygen are correct. Carbon dioxide is breathed out but this isn't an explanation, the answer is that it is made in respiration. Water vapour is also made in respiration. Always look at the action verb, like explain, to tell you how much detail to add.

Page 44

Sasha looked at the stomata in two ivy plants, she found that the plant that grew in full sunlight had less stomata. Suggest a reason for this. **AO2 (2 marks)**

If there's more light, then they need less stomata because transpiration is higher.

This answer gains 1 mark (grade B/A). The candidate correctly identified that the transpiration rate would be higher in full sun, but the first half of the sentence is information repeated from the question. To gain full marks they also need to explain that the transpiration rate is higher because water molecules have more kinetic energy as the temperature increases.*

Page 45

Explain how the structure of an artery is related to its function. **AO1 (4 marks)**

Arteries have thick walls to pump the blood and elastic fibres so they can stretch.

This answer gains 3 marks (grade D/C), as the candidate correctly identified thick walls and elastic fibres and the function of the elastic fibres. To gain full marks, they need to add that the function of the thick walls is to withstand high pressure.

Page 46

Describe the transport system in plants. **AO1 (2 marks)**

Xylem and phloem transport water and sugar.

This answer gains 0 marks (grade D/C). Although the information is correct it is not linked together properly. Xylem transports water and phloem transports sugar. Remember to be clear in your answers.

Page 47

Describe how kidneys help get rid of the body's waste products. **AO1 (4 marks)**

Kidneys clean the blood and make urea from urine. They filter the blood to get rid of the urea.

This answer gains 2 marks (grade D/C). The candidate has correctly identified urea as the waste, but missed excess water and ions. They get a mark for urine as the product. Cleaning the blood isn't scientific enough, kidneys filter the blood which they have said later on and this gets a mark. The other mark would be for saying that the kidneys reabsorb useful nutrients.

Page 48

You come across someone who is shaking and looking pale, suggest what might be wrong with them with reasons. **AO2 (3 marks)**

They are cold because they are shivering and the skin arterioles have contracted so the blood isn't by the skin, so they look pale.

This answer gains 2 marks (grade D/C). They have correctly identified that the person is cold and the reasons for being pale. To gain full marks they would need to say that shivering generates heat from the respiration needed to fuel the muscle contraction.

Page 49

Explain the reasons for deforestation. **AO1 (3 marks)**

Deforestation is the overharvesting of trees which releases carbon dioxide and can lead to global warming.

This answer gains 0 marks (grade D/C). Although the information is correct, the candidate hasn't answered the question. To achieve maximum marks, the answer should include: for timber, to make space to grow crops for food, to make space to rear livestock for food or to grow crops for biofuels.

Page 50

Explain why it is better for the environment to be a vegetarian. **AO2 (3 marks)**

Vegetarians don't eat as much so they are less wasteful and not eating beef stops the production of methane. Vegetables are the first level on a food chain so you need less land.

This answer gains 1 mark (grade D/C). The candidate has correctly identified that vegetables need less land than cattle, so it is a more efficient use of space but they also need to explain that it is because only 10% of the energy cattle get from plants is passed on. Cattle do release methane but so do rice paddies, so not eating cattle reduces the amount of methane but does not stop it. Vegetarians don't necessarily eat less so this does not get a mark.

Page 51

Give one ecological, one ethical and one health reason why it is better to eat mycoprotein than meat. **AO1 and 2 (3 marks)**

Mycoprotein doesn't involve animal cruelty, it is lower in fat and higher in protein and fibre than meat so it is healthier, and it is on the first level on a food chain so there is more energy available because it is like eating plants.

This answer gains 3 marks (grade D/C). All of the important points are covered.

Understanding the scientific process

As part of your assessment, you will need to show that you have an understanding of the scientific process – How Science Works.

This involves examining how scientific data is collected and analysed. You will need to evaluate the data by providing evidence to test ideas and develop theories. Some explanations are developed using scientific theories, models and ideas. You should be aware that there are some questions that science cannot answer and some that science cannot address.

Collecting and evaluating data

You should be able to devise a plan that will answer a scientific question or solve a scientific problem. In doing so, you will need to collect data from both primary and secondary sources. Primary data will come from your own findings – often from an experimental procedure or investigation. While working with primary data, you will need to show that you can work safely and accurately, not only on your own but also with others.

Secondary data is found by research, often using ICT – but do not forget books, journals, magazines and newspapers are also sources. The data you collect will need to be evaluated for its validity and reliability as evidence.

Presenting information

You should be able to present your information in an appropriate, scientific manner. This may involve the use of mathematical language as well as using the correct scientific terminology and conventions. You should be able to develop an argument and come to a conclusion based on recall and analysis of scientific information. It is important to use both quantitative and qualitative arguments.

Changing ideas and explanations

Many of today's scientific and technological developments have both benefits and risks. The decisions that scientists make will almost certainly raise ethical, environmental, social or economic questions. Scientific ideas and explanations change as time passes and the standards and values of society change. It is the job of scientists to validate these changing ideas.

How science ideas change

From the information you have learnt, you will know that science is a process of developing, then testing theories and models. Scientists have been carrying out this work for many centuries and it is the results of their ideas and trials that has provided us with the knowledge we have today.

However, in the process of developing this knowledge, many ideas were put forward that seem quite absurd to us today.

> During the Middle Ages, *The Miasma Theory* explained how diseases were caused. Miasma was thought to be a poisonous vapour present in the air. This vapour was said to contain particles of decaying matter that created a foul smell. The name of the killer disease malaria is derived from the Italian mala, meaning 'bad' and aria, meaning 'air'.
>
> In the nineteenth century, England was undergoing a rapid expansion of industrialisation and urbanisation. This created many foul-smelling and filthy neighbourhoods, which were focal points for disease. By improving housing, cleanliness and sanitation, levels of disease fell. This fall in the level of disease supported the miasma theory.
>
> In 1854, John Snow confirmed a cholera outbreak in London as originating from a water pump. Within ten years, Louis Pasteur was suggesting the presence of germs in substances such as milk and meat that caused them to go off quickly. He was able to remove the germs by a process we now call pasteurisation. This process is still used to protect perishable foodstuffs today.

Reliability of information

It is important to be able to spot when data or information is presented accurately, and just because you see something online or in a newspaper does not mean that it is accurate or true.

Think about what is wrong in this example, based on a newspaper report. Look at the answer at the bottom of the page to check that your observations are correct.

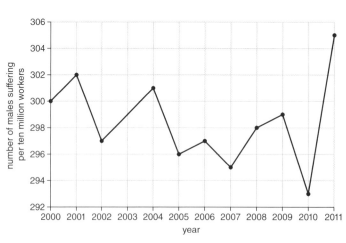

MP challenges Health Minister

The Health Minister was challenged in the House by local MP, Ralph Stag, following this week's publication of figures for the number of adult males affected by oscillatory plumbosis. Mr Stag cited this year's 'sudden and dramatic increase' in the number of sufferers and demanded swift action to discover the causes of this 'worrying trend'.

Answer

The y axis does not start at zero and so a change from 293 to 305 individuals in one year is a difference of only 12 people per ten million workers. This is unlikely to be significant and is not really a sudden and dramatic increase.

Glossary / Index

The glossary contains terms useful for your revision. Page numbers are given for items that are covered in this book.

cellulose 24 a carbohydrate; a polysaccharide used to make plant cell walls

central nervous system (CNS) 10–11, 23 collectively the brain and spinal cord

chemical reaction 6, 23, 48 process in which one or more substances are changed into other substances – chemical reactions involve rearranging atoms and energy changes

chlorophyll 17, 27, 40 green pigment inside chloroplasts in some plant cells, which absorbs energy from sunlight

cholesterol 6, 23, 45 chemical needed for the formation of cell membranes, but that increases the risk of heart disease if there is too much in the blood

chromosome 19, 24, 34–36, 40 thread-like structure in the cell nucleus that carries genetic information

climate change 50 changes in seasonal weather patterns that occur because the average temperature of Earth's surface is increasing owing to global warming

clone 20, 23, 40 group of genetically identical organisms

competition 15, 39 result of more than one organism needing the same resource, which is in short supply

compost 18 partly rotted organic material, used to improve soil for growing plants

concentration 25, 41 amount of chemical present in a given volume of a solution – usually measured as g/dm^3 or mol/dm^3

culture 9, 23 a population of microorganisms, grown on a nutrient medium

cuttings 13, 23, 40 small pieces of a plant that can grow into complete new plants

cystic fibrosis 38 a genetic disorder caused by a recessive allele, where lungs become clogged with mucus

cytoplasm 7, 24–5, 41, 46 the jelly-like material inside a cell, in which metabolic reactions take place

D

decay (biological) 18, 23, 38 the breakdown of organic material by microorganisms

denatured 30 the shape of an enzyme molecule has changed so much that it can longer bind with its substrate

dendrite 10 a short thread of cytoplasm on a neurone, carrying an impulse towards the cell body

diabetes 48 disease in which the body cannot control its blood sugar level

differentiation 35 change of a cell from general-purpose to one specialised to carry out a particular function

diffraction 25, 40, 41–42 change in the direction of a wave caused by passing through a narrow gap or round an obstacle such as a sharp corner

diffusion 25, 40, 41–42 spreading of particles of a gas, or of any substance in solution, resulting in a net movement from a region where they are in a high concentration to a region where they are in a lower concentration

digestive juices 26 liquids secreted within the digestive system and containing enzymes that help to digest food molecules

DNA 19, 35, 37 deoxyribonucleic acid – the chemical from which chromosomes are made: its sequence determines genetic characteristics, such as eye colour

dominant 36, 38 a dominant allele has an effect even when another allele is present

drug 13, 23 a chemical that changes the chemical processes in the body

drug dependency 13 feeling that you cannot manage without a drug

E

effector 10–11 part of the body that responds to a stimulus

efficiency 17 a measure of how effectively an appliance transfers the energy that flows into the appliance into useful effects

egg cell 12, 19 female gamete

embryo 12, 20, 35, 38 a very young organism, which began as a zygote and will become a fetus

embryo transplant 20, 23, 40 taking an embryo that has been produced from one female's egg and placing it into another female

energy 17, 33 the ability to 'do work'

environment 16, 29 an organism's surroundings

enzyme 7,9, 11, 25–26, 30–32, 40 biological catalyst that increases the speed of a chemical reaction but is not used up in the process

epidemic 7 many people having the same infectious disease

epidermis 27 a tissue covering the outer surface of a plant's leaf, stem or root

epithelial tissue 26, 35 tissue forming a covering over a part of an animal's body

evolution 21–22, 38 a change in a species over time

extinct 39 no longer existing

extremophile 15 an organism that can live in conditions where a particular factor, such as temperature or pH, is outside the range that most other organisms can tolerate

F

fermentation 50 process in which yeast converts sugar into ethanol (alcohol)

fertilization 12, 20 fusion of the nuclei of a male and a female gamete

fertility drug 12 hormone given to women to cause the ovaries to produce eggs

food chain 17–18, 50 flow diagram showing how energy is passed from one organism to another

fossil fuel 49 fuel such as coal, oil or natural gas, formed millions of years ago from dead plants and animals

fossil 38, 40 preserved remains of a long-dead organism

FSH 12, 23 hormone, produced by the pituitary gland, that causes eggs to mature in the ovaries

fungus (pl. fungi) 18, 24, 51 living organisms whose cells have cell walls, but that cannot photosynthesise

G

gamete 19–20 sex cell – a cell, such as an egg or sperm, containing the haploid number of chromosomes

gene 19–22, 23, 24, 35–38, 40 section of DNA that codes for a particular characteristic

genetic diagram 37, 40 a format used to describe and explain the probable results of a genetic cross

genetic engineering 21, 23 changing the genes in an organism, for example by inserting genes from another organism

genetically modified 21, 23 organism that has had genes from a different organism inserted into it

genotype 36–37 the pair of alleles that an organism possesses for a particular gene

geographical isolation 39 the separation of two populations of a species by a geographical barrier, such as a mountain chain

gland 10 organ that secretes a useful substance

glandular tissue 26, 31 tissue made up of cells that are specialised to secrete a particular substance

global warming 16, 50 gradual increase in the average temperature of Earth's surface

glucose 17, 27–28, 33, 40, 42, 47–48, 52 a simple sugar, made by plants in photosynthesis, and broken down in respiration to release energy inside all living cells

glycogen 33, 48 carbohydrate used for energy storage in animal cells

gravitropism 13, 23 a growth response to gravity

greenhouse gas 49, 52 a gas such as carbon dioxide that reduces the amount of heat escaping from Earth into space, thereby contributing to global warming

H

haemoglobin 37, 46 chemical in red blood cells which carries oxygen

HDL 6 a type of cholesterol that does not appear to cause heart disease and may help to protect against it

heart disease 6, 14 blockage of blood vessels that bring blood to the heart

herbivore 29 an animal that eats plants

heterozygous 36 possessing two different alleles of a gene

homozygous 36 possessing two identical alleles of a gene

hormones 10, 12, 23, 40 chemicals that act on target organs in the body (hormones are made by the body in special glands)

I

immune system 47 a body system that acts as a defence against pathogens, such as viruses and bacteria

immunity 8, 23, 39 you have immunity if your immune system recognises a pathogen and fights it

inoculating loop 9 metal loop that is used to transfer microorganisms

insulin 10, 21, 23, 48 hormone made by the pancreas that reduces the level of glucose in the blood

ion 11, 42 atom (or group of atoms) with a positive or negative charge, caused by losing or gaining electrons

isomerase 32 enzyme that changes glucose to fructose

IVF 12, 38 in vitro fertilisation – the fertilisation of an egg by a sperm in a glass container

K

kinetic energy 44   energy an object has because of its movement – it is greater for objects with greater mass or higher speed

L

lactic acid 33   a waste product of anaerobic respiration in muscle cells

LDL 6   a type of cholesterol that increases the risk of heart disease

LH 12, 23   hormone produced by the pituitary gland, which causes an egg to be released from an ovary

lichen 16, 23   small organism that consists of both a fungus and an alga

limiting factor 28   anything that is in short supply and therefore stops a process from happening faster

lipase 31   enzyme that breaks down fat molecules to fatty acids and glycerol molecules

lymphocyte 7   type of white blood cell

M

malnourished 6   not having a balanced diet

meiosis 34, 40   type of cell division producing four genetically different daughter cells, each with half the normal number of chromosomes

menstrual cycle 12, 23   monthly hormonal cycle that starts at puberty in human females

menstruation 12   monthly breakdown of the lining of the uterus leading to bleeding from the vagina

metabolic rate 6, 23   rate at which chemical reactions take place in the body

methane 49   the simplest hydrocarbon, CH_4 – main component of natural gas

microorganism 7, 9, 15, 18, 46   very small organism (living thing) that can be viewed only through a microscope – also known as a microbe

mitochondrion (pl: mitochondria) 24–25, 32–33, 42   organelle in which the reactions of aerobic respiration take place

mitosis 34, 40   type of cell division producing two genetically identical daughter cells

MMR 8   vaccine for measles, mumps and rubella

molecule 41   two or more atoms held together by covalent chemical bonds

motor neurone 10–11   nerve cell carrying information from the central nervous system to muscles

MRSA 8, 23   a form of the bacterium *Staphylococcus aureus* that is resistant to many antibiotics

muscular tissue 26, 35   a tissue that is specialised for contraction, causing movement

mutation 9, 22, 37   a change in the DNA in a cell

myelin sheath 10   insulating layer around a nerve fibre

N

natural selection 8, 21–22, 39, 40   the increased chance of survival of individual organisms that have phenotypes that adapt them successfully to their environment

nerve 10   group of nerve fibres

neurone 10   nerve cell

nucleus (cells) 20, 24–25   a structure found in most animal and plant cells, which contains the chromosomes made of DNA, and which controls the activities of the cell

nutrient medium 9, 23   liquid or jelly in which microorganisms can be grown

nutrient 6, 45   substance in food that we need to eat to stay healthy, such as protein

O

oestrogen 10, 12, 23   female hormone secreted by the ovary and involved in the menstrual cycle

oral contraceptive 12   pills that prevent a woman releasing eggs

organ 40   structure within an organism's body, made up of different types of tissues, that carries out a particular function

organelle 24, 40   structure within a cell

ovary 10, 12, 34   organ in a female in which eggs are made

ovulation 12   release of an egg from the ovary

oxygen debt 33   the extra oxygen that has to be taken into the body after anaerobic respiration has taken place

P

pandemic 7   when a disease spreads rapidly across many countries – perhaps the whole world

pathogen 7, 23   harmful microorganism that causes disease

pepsin 30   protease enzyme found in the stomach

pH scale 23, 30–31, 40   scale from 0 to 14 which shows how acidic or alkaline a substance is

phagocytes 7, 23   white blood cells that surround pathogens and digest them with enzymes

phenotype 36   appearance or characteristics or an organism, affected by its genes and its environment

phloem 27, 46   tissue made up of long tubes that transports sugars from the leaves to all other parts of a plant

photosynthesis 17, 19, 27–28, 32, 40, 44   process carried out by green plants where sunlight, carbon dioxide and water are used to produce glucose and oxygen

phototropism 13, 23   a growth response to light

physical factor 29, 40   something that influences a living organism that is caused by non-living aspects of their environment, such as temperature or light intensity

placebo 12   'dummy' treatment given to some patients, in a drug trial, that does not contain the drug being tested

plaque 6, 23, 45   build-up of cholesterol in a blood vessel (which may block it)

pollution 16, 23, 49   presence of substances that contaminate or damage the environment

polydactyly 38   having more than five fingers or toes on a hand or foot

progesterone 12   hormone, produced by the ovary, that prepares the uterus for pregnancy

protease 31–32   enzyme that breaks down protein molecule to amino acid molecules

protein 6, 30, 40   molecule made up of amino acids (found in food of animal origin and also in plants)

pyramid of biomass 17   a diagram in which boxes, drawn to scale, represent the biomass at each step in a food chain

Q

quadrat 29, 40   a square area within which type and numbers of living organisms can be counted or estimated

R

receptor 10–11   nerve cell that detects a stimulus

recessive 36, 38   a recessive allele only has an effect when a dominant allele is not present

reflex action 11   a fast, automatic response to a stimulus

reflex arc 11   pathway taken by nerve impulse from receptor, through nervous system, to effector

resistant strain (of bacteria) 8   a population of bacteria that is not killed by an antibiotic

respiration 19, 32, 40, 44–45   process occurring in all living cells, in which energy is released from glucose

ribosomes 24, 30   tiny structures within a cell, where protein synthesis takes place

rod cell 10   receptor cell in the eye that detects light

S

saturated fat 6   solid fat, most often of animal origin, containing no C=C double bonds

secretion 26   production and release of a useful substance

sensory neurone 10–11, 23   nerve cell carrying information from receptors to the central nervous system

sex chromosomes 36   the X and Y chromosomes

speciation 22, 39   formation of a new species

species 22, 39   group of organisms that share similar characteristics and that can breed together to produce fertile offspring

sperm 12, 19, 25, 33   male sex cell of an animal

sperm cell 12, 19, 25, 33   male gamete

starch 17–28, 31–32   a carbohydrate; a polysaccharide that is used for storing energy in plant cells, but not in animal cells

statin 14   drug that reduces cholesterol level in the blood

stem cell 35   a cell that has not yet differentiated – it can divide to form cells that form various kinds of specialised cell

sterile technique 9   handling apparatus and material to prevent microorganisms from entering them

stimulus 10–11   a change in the environment that is detected by a receptor

substrate 30   molecule on which an enzyme acts – the enzyme catalyses the reaction that changes the substrate into a product

sugar 11, 31–33, 41   sweet-tasting compound of carbon, hydrogen and oxygen such as glucose or sucrose

sweat 11, 23, 48   liquid secreted onto the skin surface that has a cooling effect as it evaporates

synapse 11   gap between two neurones

syrup 32   concentrated solution of sugar

T

target organ 10   the part of the body affected by a hormone

testes 10, 34   organs in a male in which sperms are made

thalidomide 14   a drug that was originally prescribed to pregnant women but was found to cause deformities in fetuses

tissue 26–27, 40, 46   group of cells that work together and carry out a similar task, such as lung tissue

toxin 7   poisonous substance (pathogens make toxins that make us feel ill)

tropism 13, 23   response of a plant to a stimulus, by growing towards or away from it

U

unsaturated fats 6   liquid fats, containing C=C double bonds – usually from plants or fish

V

vaccine 8, 23   killed microorganisms, or living but weakened microorganisms, that are given to produce immunity to a particular disease

vacuole 7   liquid-filled space inside a cell – many plant cells contain vacuoles full of cell sap

variation 19, 39   differences between individuals belonging to the same species

virus 7–9, 24   very small structure made of a protein coat surrounding DNA (or RNA); viruses can only reproduce inside a living cell

VO$_2$max 33   the maximum volume of oxygen the body can use per minute

W

wasted energy 17, 19, 23   energy that is transferred by a device or appliance in ways that are not wanted, or useful

wavelength 27   distance between two wave peaks

X

xylem 27, 46, 52   tissue made up of long, empty, dead cells that transports water from the roots to the leaves of a plant

Y

yeast 24   single-celled fungus used in making bread and beer

Z

zygote 30   a diploid cell formed by the fusion of the nuclei of two gametes

Collins

Workbook

NEW GCSE SCIENCE

Biology

for AQA A Higher

Authors: Gemma Young and Sarah Jinks

Revision guide +
Exam practice workbook

The key to successful revision is finding the method that suits you best. There is no right or wrong way to do it.

Before you begin, it is important to plan your revision carefully. If you have allocated enough time in advance, you can walk into the exam with confidence, knowing that you are fully prepared.

Start well before the date of the exam, not the day before!

It is worth preparing a revision timetable and trying to stick to it. Use it during the lead up to the exams and between each exam. Make sure you plan some time off too.

Different people revise in different ways and you will soon discover what works best for you.

Some general points to think about when revising

- Find a quiet and comfortable space at home where you won't be disturbed. You will find you achieve more if the room is ventilated and has plenty of light.

- Take regular breaks. Some evidence suggests that revision is most effective when tackled in 30 to 40 minute slots. If you get bogged down at any point, take a break and go back to it later when you are feeling fresh. Try not to revise when you're feeling tired. If you do feel tired, take a break.

- Use your school notes, textbook and this Revision guide.

- Spend some time working through past papers to familiarise yourself with the exam format.

- Produce your own summaries of each module and then look at the summaries in this Revision guide at the end of each module.

- Draw mind maps covering the key information on each topic or module.

- Review the Grade booster checklists on pages 117–119.

- Set up revision cards containing condensed versions of your notes.

- Prioritise your revision of topics. You may want to leave more time to revise the topics you find most difficult.

Workbook

The Workbook allows you to work at your own pace on some typical exam-style questions. You will find that the actual GCSE questions are more likely to test knowledge and understanding across topics. However, the aim of the Revision guide and Workbook is to guide you through each topic so that you can identify your areas of strength and weakness.

The Workbook also contains example questions that require longer answers (**Extended response questions**). You will find one question that is similar to these in each section of your written exam papers. The quality of your written communication will be assessed when you answer these questions in the exam, so practise writing longer answers, using sentences. The **Answers** to all the questions in the Workbook are detachable for flexible practice and can be found on pages 121–131.

At the end of the Workbook there is a series of **Revision checklists** that you can use to tick off the topics when you are confident about them and understand certain key ideas.

Remember

There is a difference between learning and revising.

When you revise, you are looking again at something you have already learned. Revising is a process that helps you to remember this information more clearly.

Learning is about finding out and understanding new information.

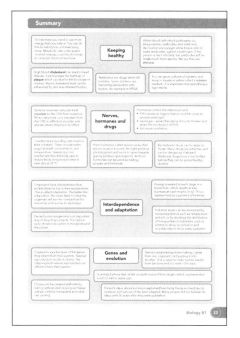

Diet and energy

1 Susan and Richard are overweight and want to lose mass. They both go on a diet and eat exactly the same food for a week. Richard loses more mass.

D–C

(a) Suggest two possible reasons why.

_____

_____

_____ [2 marks]

(b) Explain why your reasons will lead to Richard losing more mass.

_____

_____

_____ [2 marks]

2 Explain why a diet high in fat will lead to a bigger weight gain than a diet high in protein.

B–A*

fat being stored , release higher energy than protein
and not being use by anything

_____

_____ [2 marks]

Diet, exercise and health

1 Outline how high cholesterol levels in the blood can lead to a heart attack.

D–C

& Saturated fat , block bloodstream

_____

_____

_____

_____

_____

_____ [5 marks]

2 Olive oil is an unsaturated fat which can increase the amounts of HDL cholesterol in the blood. Explain why people who eat a diet high in olive oil have a low risk of developing heart disease.

B–A*

_____

_____

_____

_____ [2 marks]

Pathogens and infections

1 Explain how viruses and (bacteria) make us feel ill. → produce toxic.

reproduce, cause cell burst

[3 marks]

D–C

---

2 It was known by the mid-1800s that microorganisms caused food to go off. In the 1860s, Joseph Lister, a Scottish surgeon, in a attempt to stop so many of his patients dying from infected wounds started spraying carboxylic acid over the wounds.

(a) What was Lister's hypothesis?

[2 marks]

B–A*

(b) What evidence would he have needed to prove his hypothesis?

[1 mark]

Fighting infection

1 State two ways that lymphocytes can destroy pathogens.

produce antitoxins
antibodies.

[2 marks]

D–C

---

2 Antibodies are specific.

(a) What does this mean?

specific shape, kill specific pathogon.

[1 mark]

(b) Why does the body have to be able to produce millions of different types of lymphocytes?

[2 marks]

B–A*

Drugs against disease

1 Gita has a lung infection.

(a) Her doctor prescribes her some antibiotics. What is an antibiotic?

_____

_____ [1 mark]

D–C

(b) After 2 weeks her infection has still not cleared up. The doctor takes a swab of the mucus from her lungs and sends it to a pathology lab, so they can find out which antibiotic to give her. Explain how they would do this.

_____

_____

_____

_____

_____ [4 marks]

2 Explain why doctors are less likely to prescribe antibiotics now, compared to 40 years ago.

B–A*

_____

_____

_____

_____ [2 marks]

Antibiotic resistance

1 Explain why numbers of antibiotic-resistant bacteria have increased.

D–C

_____

_____

_____

_____

_____ [4 marks]

2 Describe and explain the trend in deaths from MRSA between 1993 and 2008.

B–A*

_____

_____

_____

_____

_____

_____ [4 marks]

Vaccination

1 The MMR vaccine is given to children in the UK.

(a) What is the function of this vaccine?

_____

_____ [1 mark]

(b) Explain how it works.

_____

_____

_____ [3 marks]

D–C

(c) In the early 21st century, the number of children having the MMR vaccine fell. State the reason for this.

_____

_____ [1 mark]

(d) The number of children having the MMR vaccine has now risen again. Explain why.

_____

_____ [1 mark]

2 Every year, elderly people are offered a flu vaccination. Suggest why they have to have a new one every year.

_____

_____

_____ [2 marks]

B–A*

Growing bacteria

1 Why is it important to grow bacteria at a temperature less than 37 °C?

_____

_____

_____ [2 marks]

D–C

2 In a industrial lab, microorganisms are kept at temperatures of around 40 °C. Suggest why.

_____

_____

_____ [2 marks]

B–A*

Co-ordination, nerves and hormones

1 What is the central nervous system (CNS)?

_____

_____ [1 mark]

2 Michelle is playing in a tennis match. Her body starts producing the hormone adrenaline, which increases her heart rate.

(a) The heart is a target organ of adrenaline. What does this mean?

_____

_____ [1 mark]

(b) Explain why a hormonal response rather than a nervous one is appropriate in this case.

_____

_____

_____

_____ [2 marks]

Receptors

1 The diagram shows a neurone.

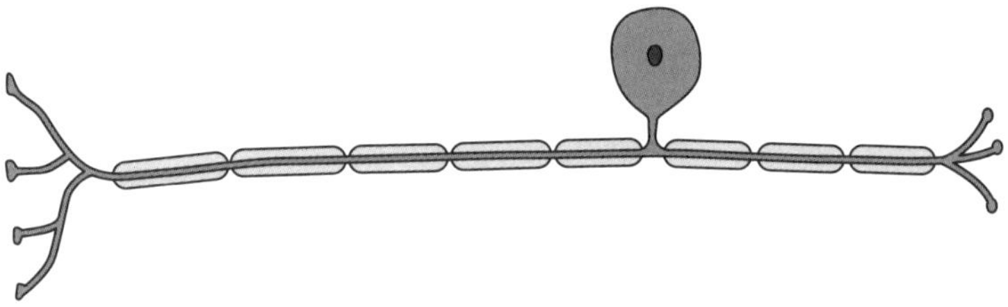

(a) What type of neurone is this?

_____

_____ [1 mark]

(b) Draw an arrow to show the direction of the message sent along this neurone. [1 mark]

(c) In what form are the messages sent?

_____

_____ [1 mark]

2 Paul is playing as a goalkeeper in a football game. The ball is heading towards him.

(a) Which receptors in his eye will be stimulated?

_____

_____ [1 mark]

(b) Describe how a picture of the ball is constructed by his brain.

_____

_____

_____

_____

_____ [3 marks]

Reflex actions

1 Your finger touches a sharp pin. Almost immediately, your finger moves away. Describe the sequence of events that has happened to bring this about.

_____

_____

_____

_____

_____

D–C

[6 marks]

2 You grab onto a hot radiator to stop you from falling over. Ordinarily, you would have pulled away from the radiator in a reflex action but your brain has overridden this.

(a) What kind of control is you brain carrying out?

_____

_____

[1 mark]

B–A*

(b) Explain why your brain has made this decision.

_____

_____

[1 mark]

Controlling the body

1 Why is it important that human body temperature is maintained at around 37 °C?

_____

_____

_____

[2 marks]

D–C

2 If you are stranded in a desert, you should avoid exertion. Explain why.

_____

_____

_____

_____

_____

_____

[4 marks]

B–A*

Reproductive hormones

1 Explain how the oestrogen in the contraceptive pill stops a woman from getting pregnant.

_____

_____

_____

_____

_____ [3 marks]

2 Use the image below to explain how the level of oestrogen affects events in the menstrual cycle.

_____

_____

_____

_____

_____

_____

_____ [3 marks]

Controlling fertility

1 Outline the stages in IVF.

_____

_____

_____

_____

_____ [3 marks]

2 The number of triplets being born in the UK has risen in the last century. Ruby thinks this is due to more women using fertility drugs.

(a) Explain why her hypothesis could be correct.

_____

_____

_____ [2 marks]

(b) Use what you know about the dangers of multiple births to suggest another hypothesis for this trend.

_____

_____

_____ [2 marks]

Plant responses and hormones

1 Tropisms can be positive or negative. Complete each of these statements with the correct word.

    (a) A shoot growing towards the light is _____ phototropism.   [1 mark]

    (b) A shoot growing away from gravity is _____ gravitropism.   [1 mark]

D–C

2 You are asked to test the hypothesis: The tip of the shoot detects the direction of light.

    (a) Write a plan which will enable you to do this.

    _____

    _____

    _____

    _____

    _____   [3 marks]

    (b) Describe what you will see if the hypothesis is correct.

    _____

    _____   [2 marks]

B–A*

Drugs

1 **(a)** Name a recreational drug that is:

    (i) legal _____

    (ii) illegal _____   [2 marks]

    (b) Explain why it is difficult to stop smoking.

    _____

    _____

    _____   [2 marks]

D–C

2 State two ways a person could die from alcohol consumption.

    _____

    _____

    _____   [2 marks]

B–A*

Developing new drugs

1 The table of data shows the results from a double-blind trial of a flu drug called zanamivir.

	given zanamivir	given a placebo
number of subjects	293	295
mean age in years	19	19
number of days until their temperature went down to normal	2.00	2.33
number of days until they lost all their symptoms and felt better	3.00	2.83
number of days until they felt just as well as before they had flu	4.5	6.3
average score the volunteers gave to their experience of the major symptoms of flu	23.4	25.3

TABLE 1: Effect of zanamivir and a placebo on soldiers suffering from flu

(a) What is meant by a 'double-blind' trial?

_____

_____ [3 marks]

(b) State one control variable in the trial.

_____ [1 mark]

(c) Use the data to state one reason why the drug should be distributed.

_____ [1 mark]

D–C

2 When statins were first trialled they showed no side-effects. However, since then, side-effects have been discovered. Explain why they did not discover the side-effects in the trials.

_____

_____ [4 marks]

B–A*

Legal and illegal drugs

1 Study the data below and use it to answer the questions that follow.

Year	2000	2001	2002	2003	2004	2005	2006	2007	2008
Men	4483	4938	5069	5443	5431	5566	5768	5732	5999
Women	2401	2561	2632	2721	2790	2820	2990	2992	3032

TABLE 2: The number of deaths from drinking alcohol, in each year from 2000 to 2008, in England and Wales.

(a) Describe two trends as seen in the data.

_____

_____ [2 marks]

(b) Heroin is considered a much more dangerous drug than alcohol. There were around 900 deaths from heroin in 2008. Describe how this compares with the deaths from alcohol and explain the reason for the difference.

_____

_____ [2 marks]

D–C

2 State two reasons why professional sportspeople should not take performance-enhancing drugs.

_____

_____ [2 marks]

B–A*

Competition

1 Suzanne is growing vegetables on her allotment. Explain to her why it is important for her to remove weeds.

_____

_____

_____ [2 marks]

D–C

2 Flamingos are able to feed in lakes that are so alkaline that almost nothing else can survive there – except the shrimps and small aquatic insects that they eat. Explain how this increases their chances of having offspring.

_____

_____

_____

_____

_____ [3 marks]

B–A*

Adaptations for survival

1 Images of a wasp and a hoverfly are shown here.

(a) Wasps can sting. How does this help them to survive?

wasp   hoverfly

_____

_____ [1 mark]

D–C

(b) The hoverfly cannot sting. Explain why it looks like the wasp.   *warning colour*

_____

_____

_____ [2 marks]

2 Explain how the discovery of extremophiles on Earth has led scientists to believe that finding life on the planet Mars is possible.

_____

_____

_____

_____

_____ [2 marks]

B–A*

Environmental change

1 Cockatoos are birds that live in central Australia. They feed on seeds and fruit. Global warming has caused rainfall in their habitat to decrease. Explain how this will affect the cockatoo population.

D–C

_____

_____

_____

_____

_____ [3 marks]

2 (a) Predict how the fall in numbers of honeybees will affect food prices in the UK.

_____

_____ [1 mark]

B–A*

(b) Explain your prediction.

_____

_____

_____ [2 marks]

Pollution indicators

1 Cathy works for the Environmental Agency. Her job is to monitor pollution levels. She wants to measure the amount of dissolved oxygen in a stream.

(a) State the instrument she could use to do this.

_____ [1 mark]

(b) She finds high levels of oxygen. What does this tell her about the level of pollution in the stream?

_____

_____ [1 mark]

D–C

(c) Give one example of an invertebrate she may find in the stream and explain how this is a further indicator of the pollution levels in the water.

_____

_____

_____ [2 marks]

2 Bloodworms are red in colour because they contain high levels of haemoglobin, the pigment found in red blood cells. Explain how this adaptation allows them to survive in polluted water.

B–A*

_____

_____

_____ [2 marks]

Food chains and energy flow

1 Only a small amount of the energy from light falling on a plant is used for photosynthesis.
State one reason for this.

_____

_____ [1 mark]

D–C

2 (a) A plant is 10% efficient. Use the formula:

$$\text{efficiency} = \frac{\text{useful energy transferred}}{\text{original amount of energy}} \times 100\%$$

to calculate how many units of energy are used in photosynthesis if 800 units hit the leaf.

_____

_____ [2 marks]

B–A*

(b) Explain why plants that grow in shady places usually have bigger leaves.

_____

_____

_____

_____ [2 marks]

Biomass

1 Sketch a pyramid of biomass for the following food chain: Grass → rabbit → fox

D–C

[2 marks]

2 Explain why food chains in the ocean are often much longer than food chains on land.

_____

_____

_____

_____

_____ [3 marks]

B–A*

Decay

1 June has a compost heap in her garden.

D–C

(a) In the summer, she waters the compost. Why?

_____

_____

_____ [3 marks]

(b) What is the function of the air slats at the bottom?

_____

_____ [2 marks]

(c) She puts the compost onto her plants. Why?

_____

_____ [2 marks]

B–A*

2 When food is canned it is added to a tin, sealed and then heated to a high temperature. Explain how this stops the food inside from decaying.

_____

_____

_____ [3 marks]

Recycling

D–C

1 To the food chain below, add a label and arrows to show the role of microorganisms. [2 marks]

B–A*

2 Explain the roles of scavengers, such as crabs and microorganisms, in the recycling of nutrients in a community.

_____

_____

_____ [2 marks]

The carbon cycle

1 This diagram of the carbon cycle shows how carbon is recycled around the Earth.

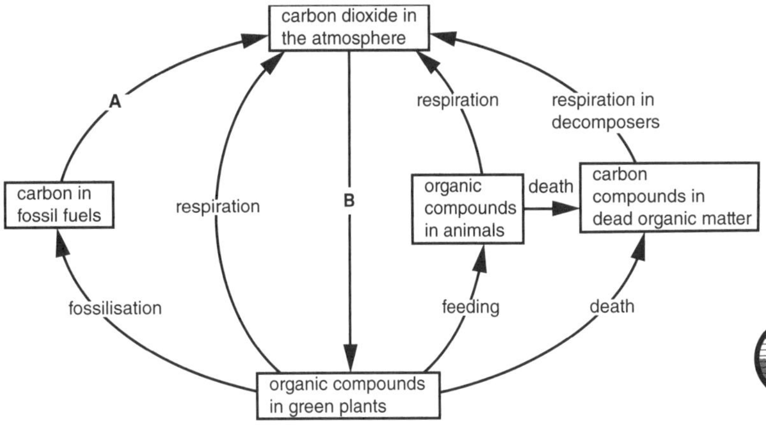

(a) Name the process missing in:

(i) A _____

(ii) B _____

[2 marks]

(b) Animals need carbon in order to build tissue. How do they get the carbon they need?

_____

_____ [1 mark]

Diagram labels:
- carbon dioxide in the atmosphere
- respiration
- respiration in decomposers
- A
- carbon in fossil fuels
- respiration
- B
- organic compounds in animals
- death
- carbon compounds in dead organic matter
- fossilisation
- feeding
- death
- organic compounds in green plants

(c) A carbon atom that makes up the muscle of an animal will one day return to the atmosphere. Explain how this will happen.

_____

_____

_____ [4 marks]

2 (a) State the energy transfer that takes place in each of these stages of the carbon cycle:

(i) photosynthesis _____ [2 marks]

(ii) combustion of wood. _____ [2 marks]

(b) Explain how some of the energy stored in food ends up as movement energy.

_____ [2 marks]

Genes and chromosomes

1 Sanjay has genes for blood group A and blood group O. Explain how he got two genes for his blood group.

_____ [2 marks]

2 Leanne picked 10 leaves from two different holly bushes. She measured the length of the leaves. Her results are shown in the table below:

Bush	Length of leaves (mm)
A	64, 59, 76, 56, 72, 68, 73, 77, 58, 64
B	76, 81, 82, 65, 59, 62, 59, 80, 74, 81

(a) Calculate the mean leaf length for each bush. _____ [2 marks]

(b) Why did she measure 10 leaves from each bush and not just one?

_____ [1 mark]

(c) State reasons for the difference in mean leaf length.

_____ [2 marks]

Reproduction

1 This single-celled organism is reproducing by dividing into two.

(a) What type of reproduction is this?

_____ [1 mark]

(b) The offspring will be a clone of its parent. Why?

_____ [1 mark]

(c) Explain why the offspring of animals are different from their parents.

_____

_____ [1 mark]

D–C

---

2 (a) State the difference between internal and external fertilisation.

_____

_____ [2 marks]

(b) Most fish use external fertilisation. Explain why female fish produce thousands of eggs at a time.

_____

_____ [2 marks]

B–A*

Cloning plants and animals

1 Margaret has successfully bred an award-winning plant. She wants to clone it.

(a) Why does she want to clone it?

_____

_____ [2 marks]

(b) State one method she can use and explain how to carry it out.

_____

_____

_____ [3 marks]

D–C

---

2 The Pyrenean ibex, a form of wild mountain goat, was officially declared extinct in 2000 but scientists have preserved tissue samples and can use this to create clones.

(a) Explain why scientists want to clone it.

_____

_____ [1 mark]

(b) Outline the process that could be used to clone the ibex.

_____

_____

_____

_____

_____ [4 marks]

B–A*

Genetic engineering

1 Human insulin can be produced by bacteria grown in huge vats.

(a) Why are these bacteria known as a GM organisms?

_____

_____ [1 mark]

(b) Outline the procedure used to make GM bacteria that are able to produce human insulin.

_____

_____

_____

_____ [3 marks]

(c) The culture inside the vat has to be maintained at a temperature of around 37 °C. Why?

_____

_____

_____ [2 marks]

D–C

---

2 A type of GM cotton plant called Bt cotton produces a toxin in its leaves which kills any insect pests that feed on it.

(a) Explain why farmers may want to grow Bt cotton instead of normal cotton.

_____

_____

_____

_____ [3 marks]

(b) State one reason why people may be worried about farms growing Bt cotton.

_____

_____ [1 mark]

B–A*

Evolution

1 Lamarck stated that as a giraffe stretches up to eat leaves from a high tree, its neck gets longer. This characteristic would be passed on to the next generation. Use what you know about how characteristics are inherited to explain why we know this is not true.

_____

_____

_____ [3 marks]

D–C

---

2 'Evolution means that eventually all organisms will become more complex.' Discuss evidence for and against this statement.

_____

_____

_____ [3 marks]

B–A*

Natural selection

1 (a) Peppered moths are a pale colour. They like to rest on the trunks of trees. How does the colour of the moth help it to survive?

_____

_____ [2 marks]

(b) Occasionally there is a mutation and a black moth is born. What is a mutation?

_____ [1 mark]

(c) In the past, air pollution in the UK caused the bark of the trees to turn black. Explain how this meant that the numbers of black moths increased.

_____

_____

_____ [3 marks]

D–C

2 Warfarin can be used as a rat poison. The number of rats that are resistant to warfarin is increasing. Philippa thinks this is because when the rats come into contact with warfarin their body figures out a way of becoming resistant. Explain to her what really happens.

_____

_____

_____ [3 marks]

B–A*

Evidence for evolution

1 The bones in the arms of birds, bats and humans are shown here.

(a) Why are they all slightly different?

_____

_____ [1 mark]

(b) Explain how this is evidence for evolution.

_____

_____

_____

_____ [3 marks]

bat wing

human arm

bird wing

D–C

2 This evolutionary tree includes four of the major classification groups.

(a) Do animals have more features in common with bacteria or archaea? Explain how you know.

_____

_____ [2 marks]

(b) What is represented by the question mark?

_____

_____ [2 marks]

animals

archaea

fungi

bacteria

plants

?

B–A*

Extended response question

As a seedling grows, it is important that its roots become anchored in the ground. Use what you know about how auxins control cell growth to explain how this happens.

The quality of written communication will be assessed in your answer to this question.

_____

_____

_____

_____

_____

_____

_____

_____

_____

_____

_____

_____

_____

_____

_____

_____

_____

_____

_____

_____

_____

_____

_____

_____

_____

_____

_____

_____

_____

_____

_____

_____

_____

_____ [6 marks]

Animal and plant cells

1 (a) What type of cell is shown in the diagram?

_____ [1 mark]

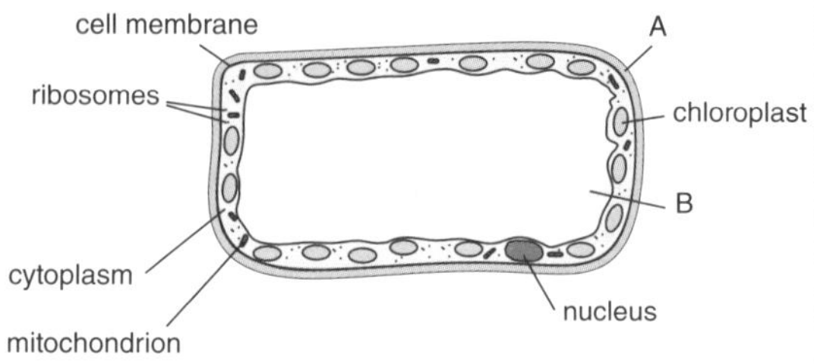

(b) Name the missing organelles A and B.

_____

_____ [2 marks]

(c) State the function of the ribosomes.

_____

_____ [1 mark]

what it's used for.

(d) Explain why leaf cells contain many (chloroplasts) but root cells contain none.

_____

_____

_____

_____ [3 marks]

D–C

Diagram labels: cell membrane, ribosomes, cytoplasm, mitochondrion, A, chloroplast, B, nucleus

2 Explain why a scientist studying viruses would use an electron microscope rather than a light microscope.

① small

② need to be magnified many times.

③. electron microscope magnified more than

_____ [3 marks]

B–A*

Microbial cells

1 State one similarity and one difference between:

(a) a plant cell and yeast.

cell wall , cytoplasm, mitocondria.

ribosome.

chloroplast, vacuole. , made of cellulose / [2 marks]

chitin.

(b) an animal cell and bacteria.

cytoplasm, cell membrane.

no nucleus // mitochondria [2 marks]

D–C

2 The smallest virus has a diameter of 0.02 µm. How many of these viruses could fit end to end across the diameter of a typical animal cell (diameter 20 µm)?

_____ [1 mark]

B–A*

Diffusion

1 A cake is cooking in the kitchen. Use ideas about diffusion to explain how the smell travels around the house.

caused by molecules
transfer from high conc to kitchen bw conc. in house
until all the molecules are evenly distributed

[4 marks]

D–C

2 Glucose diffuses from the blood into cells where it is used for respiration.

(a) State how the concentration of glucose is kept low inside the cells.

keep be using up by respiration.

[1 mark]

(b) Why is it important that the glucose concentration is kept low in the cells?

blood keeps high.
keep diffusing in.

[2 marks]

B–A*

(c) This equipment was left for an hour. The inside of the visking tubing was then tested for the presence of glucose. Predict the results and explain why you think this will happen.

[3 marks]

glucose solution

Visking tubing

distilled (pure) water

Specialised cells

1 State one adaptation of a red blood cell and explain why it has this adaptation.

[2 marks]

D–C

2 Root hair cells are a specialised root cell. State how they are adapted and explain why they have this adaptation.

[3 marks]

B–A*

Tissues

1 (a) What type of tissue is shown in the diagram?

_____ [1 mark]

(b) Explain why this tissue contains many mitochondria.

respia respaire

give energy

contrust _____ [2 marks]

D-C

2 This diagram shows the human lungs.

(a) Name the process by which oxygen moves across the air sacs and into the bloodstream.

_____ [1 mark]

(b) Suggest how the airs sacs increase the efficiency of this process.

increase the surface area

_____ [1 mark]

B-A*

(c) Explain why getting oxygen to where it is needed is a simpler process in bacteria than it is in humans.

Simple

complecuted structures, oxyge-

travel qround to reuch every organ. [2 marks]

lung

air sacs

Animal tissues and organs

1 Match the digestive system organ to its function.

	Organ			Function
1	stomach A		A	contractions of muscle in walls mixes food with digestive juices
2	liver D		B	produces digestive juices
3	small intestine E		C	is where water is absorbed from the undigested food, producing faeces
4	pancreas B		D	produces bile
5	large intestine C		E	is where the absorption of soluble food occurs

_____ [5 marks]

D-C

2 Explain the function of the epithelial cells which line the inside of the small intestine.

cover and protect the linning from

cligestive juice,

lubricunt, pass easily.

produce muscus [4 marks]

B-A*

Plant tissues and organs

1 The diagram shows a cross-section of a leaf.

(a) State the function of each of these tissues:

(i) upper epidermis

cover ,
① protect, underlying cell
② prevent lose too much water [2 marks]

(ii) mesophyll.

chloroplast, photosynthesis. [1 mark]

(b) Name the tissue that carries water to the leaves.

xylem [1 mark]

D–C

2 (a) The lower epidermis of the leaf contains tiny holes called stomata. What is their function?

gas exchange. water control. [1 mark]

(b) In hot conditions the stomata may close. Suggest why.

not enough water, prevent water loss. [1 mark]

B–A*

Photosynthesis

1 Tyrone kept some geranium plants in a dark cupboard for two days. He then added iodine to their leaves. Iodine turns black if it comes into contact with starch.

(a) Predict what he would see.

Become nothing [1 mark]

(b) Explain the reasons behind your prediction.

no photosynthesis
can't produce starch glucose
glucose can't -> starch [3 marks]

(c) He also tested the leaves of some variegated (green and white) geranium leaves that had been kept in a sunny place. This is what he saw.
Explain why he got these results.

ribosome in middle.
most protein synthesi.
chloroplast in middle,
most glucse produce. [4 marks]
starch only store in middle, iodine contact with starch

went black

stayed orange

D–C

2 Why does chlorophyll look green?

[3 marks]

B–A*

Limiting factors

1 An experiment was set up as shown in the diagram. The lamp was moved towards the plant and the average number of bubbles released by the plant per minute were counted, averaged and recorded at each distance. The results are shown in the table below.

collected gas
inverted test tube
bubbles of gas
beaker
water
inverted funnel
water-weed

(a) Name the gas in the bubbles.

_____ [1 mark]

(b) Use the results to describe how light intensity affects the rate of photosynthesis.

_____ [1 mark]

D–C

(c) Describe what happens to the rate of photosynthesis once the lamp gets closer than 15 cm away.

_____ [1 mark]

(d) Explain why this has happened.

① no longer limited effect

② another factor is   [2 marks]
limiting CO_2.

Distance between the lamp and plant (cm)	50	45	40	35	30	25	20	15	10	5
Number of bubbles of oxygen released per minute	1	2	5	10	16	32	54	56	56	56

2 Greenhouses are used to increase the rate of photosynthesis of the plants growing inside.

(a) Suggest how tomatoes grown inside a greenhouse would compare to those grown outside.

_____ [1 mark]

(b) A greenhouse has a heater and an automatic watering system. Explain how each of these maximises the rate of photosynthesis of the plants growing inside.

_____
_____ [2 marks]

B–A*

(c) Suggest one more addition to the greenhouse that would increase photosynthesis even more.

_____ [1 mark]

The products of photosynthesis

1 Peas are high in protein. Explain how the pea plant makes this protein.

photosynthesis → glucose.
Nitrate ions → absorb from root
react to form   [3 marks]

D–C

glucose, sucrose, starch, protein,
cellulae, fat + oil

2 The seeds of the dandelion plant are dispersed by the wind. The seeds contain oil as a store of energy.

(a) Why do the seeds need a store of energy?

For the plant embryo to grow,   [1 mark]

B–A*

(b) Explain why oil is a good choice for the energy store in the seed.

not dissolve in water.
contain high amount of energy per gram   [2 marks]
→ light, easily dispersed by wind

Distribution of organisms

1 Explain why the distribution of:

(a) plants in a cave is low

___① not enough ~~oxyge co~~, light for ②photosynthew___
___②for growth___ [2 marks] **D–C**

(b) egg wrack seaweed at the top of a beach, far from the sea, is low.

___① stay where there is enough water .___
___② otherwise dry out.___ [2 marks]

2 The grey squirrel was introduced from North America to the UK at the end of the 19th century. In England, red squirrels are now only found in a few places.

(a) Describe how the distribution of red and grey squirrels has changed in the UK since the end of the 19th century.

_____

_____ [1 mark] **B–A***

(b) The grey squirrels are better adapted than the red squirrels. Use this to explain the changes in distribution.

___competitor , ~~easier to~~ survive,,___
___win___
___die.___ [3 marks]

Using quadrats to sample organisms

1 Rory wanted to estimate the number of snails on his lawn. He threw a quadrat onto it. You can see the result on the right.

(a) Rory's lawn has an area of 2 m². Estimate how many snails there are on the entire lawn.

_____ [2 marks]

(b) Explain how he could increase the validity of his results.

___randomly several time___
___calculate.___ [2 marks]

D–C

2 A scientist wanted to work out what size quadrat would be best to use to estimate the distribution of different plants growing in a field. She tried different sizes and counted how many different species she could count inside each one. She then drew a graph of her results.
She chose a size of 15 cm. Explain why.

___① reasonably high number___
___② large can caught more___
___③ But hard to count___

_____ [3 marks]

B–A*

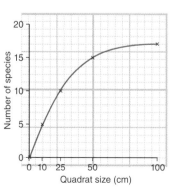

1 The image below represents part of a protein molecule.

D–C

(a) What are the individual units called?

_____ [1 mark]

(b) Why is it important that these units are arranged in the correct order?

_____

_____ [2 marks]

B–A*

2 You eat a meal high in protein. Explain how your body uses this protein to form muscle protein in your leg.

_____

_____

_____

_____

_____ [5 marks]

Enzymes

1 Emma carried out an investigation where she added amylase to starch and measured how long it took before all the starch disappeared. She repeated the experiment at different temperatures.

(a) In this reaction what is the:

(i) substrate?

_____ [1 mark]

D–C

(ii) product?

_____ [1 mark]

(b) Name her independent variable.

_____ [1 mark]

(c) State one control variable she should use.

_____ [1 mark]

2 The graph shows Emma's results. Explain the shape of the graph.

_____

_____

_____

B–A*

_____

_____

_____

_____ [6 marks]

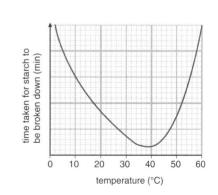

Enzymes and digestion

1 Fill in the gaps in the table. [6 marks]

Enzyme group	Substrate	Product	Where enzyme is produced
amylase	(a)_____	sugars	(b)_____ glands in the mouth and pancreas
(c)_____	protein	amino acids	pancreas, (d)_____ and small intestine
(e)_____	lipids (fats and oils)	fatty acids and (f)_____	pancreas and small intestine

D–C

2 (a) Use the graph to state the optimum pH of the enzyme amylase.

_____ [1 mark]

(b) Amylase breaks down starch in the small intestine. The food that enters the small intestine is acidic because it has mixed with the digestive juices in the stomach.

(i) Explain why the digestive juices in the stomach are acidic.

_____ [1 mark]

(ii) Explain how the pH of the small intestine is kept at the optimum pH for amylase. _____

_____

_____ [3 marks]

B–A*

Enzymes at home

1 (a) Harry was eating a greasy burger and spilt fat down his T-shirt. Explain why washing it in biological washing powder will help remove the fat stain.

_____

_____ [3 marks]

(b) He decided to wash the T-shirt at 60 °C to make sure the stain came out. Explain why this is not a good idea.

_____

_____ [3 marks]

D–C

2 Susie wanted to test the hypothesis that biological detergents break down keratin in the skin. She decided to use egg white instead of keratin. Egg white contains the protein albumin.

(a) Write a simple method that she could use to test the hypothesis. State what results she will get if the hypothesis is correct.

_____

_____

_____ [4 marks]

(b) You could argue that her method will lead to results which are not valid. Explain why.

_____ [1 mark]

B–A*

Enzymes in industry

1 Manufacturers of sports drinks often make sugar syrup for their drinks from starch solution.

(a) State how they turn the starch solution into sugar syrup.

_____ [1 mark]

(b) Why don't they just use sugar syrup?

_____ [1 mark]

D–C

(c) Explain why slimming foods may contain fructose instead of glucose.

_____

_____ [3 marks]

(d) Name the enzyme used to turn glucose into fructose.

_____ [1 mark]

---

2 Bees produce an enzyme called sucrase which they use to produce honey from nectar. Nectar is high in sucrose.

(a) State what two sugars are found in honey.

_____

_____ [2 marks]

B–A*

(b) State one use of sucrase in the food industry.

_____ [1 mark]

Aerobic respiration

1 (a) Why do all your cells need a supply of oxygen?

_____

_____ [2 marks]

D–C

(b) Describe how oxygen from the air reaches all your cells.

_____

_____ [2 marks]

---

2 The amount of oxygen and carbon dioxide absorbed by the leaves of a tree was measured over a day in December.
The results are shown in the diagram.
Explain the shape of the graph.

B–A*

_____

_____

_____

_____

_____

_____

_____ [6 marks]

Using energy

1 If you use more energy than you take in you will lose body mass.

(a) Andrew goes running every day. How does this help him to lose body mass?

_____

_____ [2 marks]

(b) Explain how running on a cold day will help him to lose more mass.

_____

_____ [2 marks]

D–C

2 Explain why muscle cells in the heart contain a lot of mitochondria.

_____

_____

_____

_____

_____ [3 marks]

B–A*

Anaerobic respiration

1 (a) State two reasons why it is more beneficial for cells to carry out aerobic respiration than anaerobic.

_____

_____ [2 marks]

(b) Alice has just completed a sprint race. For a few minutes afterwards she continues to breathe deeply and at a fast rate. Explain why.

_____

_____ [2 marks]

D–C

2 Tom is in training for a swimming championship.

(a) Why does he want to increase his VO_2 max?

_____ [1 mark]

(b) This graph shows the VO_2 max for different sports people. Use it to inform him which sport would be best for him to take up in order to improve his VO_2 max.

_____ [1 marks]

(c) Explain how taking up this sport will increase his chances of winning the swimming races.

_____

_____

_____

_____ [3 marks]

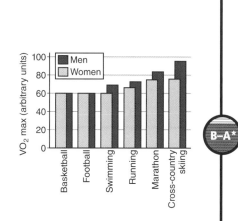

B–A*

Cell division – mitosis

1 Describe why:

(a) mitosis results in <u>two daughter</u> cells.

full set copy of gene, gene duplicated. identical to each other.

[1 mark]

(b) the daughter cells are genetically identical to the parent cell.

full set of copy

[1 mark]

(c) skin cells frequently undergo mitosis.

to repair & replace

[1 mark]

D–C

2 The diagram shows the stages that happen during mitosis.

(a) Describe what has happened to the chromosomes between stages A and B.

DNA duplicated.

[1 mark]

A B C D

(b) Explain what is happening in stages C and D.

mitosis, cells divided into two

[2 marks]

B–A*

Cell division – meiosis

1 A horse has 64 chromosomes in its body cells. This diagram shows the stages that happen during meiosis in a female horse.

(a) Where in the female horse's body does meiosis take place?

[1 mark]

(b) State the number of chromosomes in each of the numbered cells.

[3 marks]

(c) Explain why meiosis is essential for (successful) sexual reproduction.

① number of gamete is half of full set

[2 marks]

D–C

① parent cell

② ③

④ ⑤ ⑥ ⑦ daughter cells

2 Outline the differences and similarities between mitosis and meiosis.

① identical / fertilisation.
② fertilisation body cell / gamate
③ 4 / 2.
④ half / full

[4 marks]

B–A*

Stem cells

1 Parkinson's disease is caused by the death of cells in the brain. Explain how stem cells could be used in the future to treat it.

_from embyo/adult ____ ____ _____

underline: _unspecialised cell → differenciate to carry out specific function →_

[3 marks]

2 You see a website advertising a cure for blindness using stem cell therapy in a clinic in China. Outline reasons why people should be cautious about going there for treatment.

[3 marks]

Genes, alleles and DNA

1 DNA fingerprinting can be used to find out who a child's father is. Use the DNA fingerprint below to:

(a) state who the father is.

[1 mark]

(b) explain how the DNA fingerprint is evidence that he is the father.

[2 marks]

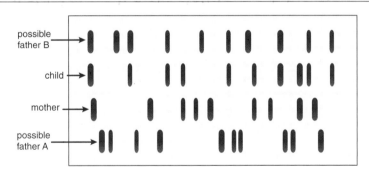

2 BRCA1 and BRCA2 are genes that belong to a class of genes known as tumour suppressors. Some people carry a mutation in these genes.

(a) Describe two trends as shown on the graph.

[2 marks]

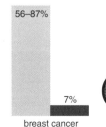

(b) Carly is 35. Both her mother and grandmother died of breast cancer. Explain why she is also at high risk from developing it.

interest

[2 marks]

Mendel

1 Explain why scientists did not accept Mendel's ideas until after his death.

D–C

· how characteristic's inherit.

not a scientist , obscure journal

~~similar, more acceptable publish~~ [1 mark]

2 One experiment that Mendel carried out involved breeding together short and tall pea plants. At the time it was widely believed that all characteristics from parents were blended in the offspring.

(a) Use the blending theory to predict the outcome of a cross between a tall pea plant and a short one.

_____ [1 mark]

B–A*

(b) Mendel carried out this cross and discovered that all the offspring were tall. Explain why.

tall —> dominant allele.

determine by dominant

carry the recessive one [3 marks]

How genes affect characteristics

1 (a) Natasha has two alleles for hair colour. Why has she got two?

_____ [1 mark]

D–C

(b) She has blonde hair. The blonde hair allele (b) is recessive. What pair of alleles has she got?

_____ [1 mark]

(c) Her friend Nisha has brown hair. The brown hair allele is dominant over the blonde hair allele. What possible alleles has Nisha got?

_____

_____ [2 marks]

2 Some androgens control the development of an embryo so it becomes male. On which chromosome are the genes for these hormones found? Explain your answer.

B–A*

X, only male

_____

_____ [2 marks]

Inheriting chromosomes and genes

1 A long-haired guinea pig was bred with a short-haired one and produced 12 short-haired offspring.

(a) Which allele is most likely to be dominant?

_____ [1 mark]

(b) What alleles will the offspring have?

_____ [1 mark]

(c) Draw a genetic diagram to show the cross between one of the offspring and a long-haired guinea pig.

D–C

[3 marks]

(d) What is the ratio of homozygous to heterozygous genotypes?

_____ [1 mark]

2 Pea seeds can either be yellow or green. Green is the dominant allele. A grower wanted to find out the genotype of a plant that produces green seeds. Explain how he could use a test cross to find this out.

_____

_____

_____ [3 marks]

B–A*

How genes work

1 Erin has brown eyes. She inherited the brown eye allele from her mother. Describe how this allele produces brown eyes.

_____

_____

_____

_____ [4 marks]

D–C

2 Joshua suffers from type 1 diabetes, which means his body cannot produce insulin. Explain how this could have been caused by a mutation.

_____ Order of the base of DNA changed. _____

_____ code _____

_____ [2 marks]

B–A*

Genetic disorders

1 This diagram shows an example of a family tree for cystic fibrosis.

(a) What genotype does person E have?

_____ [1 mark]

(b) Explain why people A and B must be carriers of the cystic fibrosis allele.

_____

_____

_____ [2 marks]

(c) Calculate the probability of person D also being a carrier of cystic fibrosis.

_____ [1 mark]

normal female ◯

female with cystic fibrosis ◯ (shaded)

normal male ▢

male with cystic fibrosis ▢ (shaded)

2 Tay–Sachs disease is a fatal recessive genetic disorder. Children who are born with it usually die by the age of four.
Louise and Stuart's daughter died of the disease. They want to try for another baby. Describe how embryo screening can be used to enable them to have a child free of the disease.

_____

_____

_____

_____ [3 marks]

Fossils

1 The bodies of jellyfish are very soft. They have no bones. Explain why scientists have very little evidence of how jellyfish evolved.

Soft part decayed
Do not fossil well
no evidence from ages ago.

_____ [3 marks]

2 A scientist found what he believed to be the oldest fossil ever found on a beach in western Australia. He dated it at 3.43 billion years old. It seemed to show tubular structures shaped like bacteria, which could be the common ancestor of all life on Earth.

(a) State one piece of evidence, other than the fossil, that leads scientists to believe that all life on Earth is descended from a common ancestor.

_____

_____ [1 mark]

(b) Scientists have many theories as to how life on Earth evolved. What is needed to prove one of these theories correct?

_____

_____ [2 marks]

Extinction

1 The Croatian dace is a small fish found only in one small stream in Croatia. People introduced trout into the stream. State two possible reasons why Croatian dace are in danger of becoming extinct.

Can't adapted and mutate quick enough

predator

[2 marks]

D–C

2 Around 65 million years ago a mass extinction occurred. Scientists believe it was due to a massive meteorite hitting the Earth, throwing dust into the air. This blocked the heat from the Sun reaching the surface of the Earth.

(a) What do we mean by a mass extinction?

high numbers of species become extinct over a short period of time.

[2 marks]

(b) What evidence do scientists have that a mass extinction happened at this time?

high

[1 mark]

B–A*

(c) The meteorite caused the extinction of the dinosaurs but other species such as small mammals survived. Suggest why.

[2 marks]

New species

1 Charles Darwin visited the Galapagos Islands off the coast of South America. He found that on each island there was a different species of finch. We now know that they all descended from one species found on the mainland. Explain the process that led to the evolution of these many different species of finch.

[5 marks]

D–C

2 In one area of a field the soil is contaminated with toxic metals. The type of grass growing in this area starts to evolve to cope with the metals. It also evolves a new flowering time. The grass in the rest of the field remains as it is. Explain how this means that there is a new species of grass in the field.

mutate & adapted to

Can't breed

not same Time,

can't breed means not same species

[3 marks]

B–A*

Extended response question

Control systems are used to keep human temperature at around 37 °C. Explain why it is dangerous for our body temperature to go much higher. Use what you know about enzymes in your answer.

The quality of written communication will be assessed in your answer to this question.

_____
_____
_____
_____
_____
_____
_____
_____
_____
_____
_____
_____
_____
_____
_____
_____
_____
_____
_____
_____
_____
_____
_____
_____
_____
_____
_____
_____
_____
_____
_____
_____
_____
_____
_____
_____
_____ [6 marks]

Osmosis

1 Visking tubing can be used to demonstrate osmosis.

(a) What property of visking tubing makes it useful for demonstrating osmosis?

_____ [1 mark]

(b) Which two things are needed for osmosis to take place?

_____ [2 marks]

D–C

2 In a series of experiments visking tubing filled with a solution of 1% sodium chloride solution is placed into beakers with various concentrations (as shown in the table).

Experiment	Visking tubing solution	Beaker solution
1	1% NaCl	0.5% NaCl
2	1% NaCl	1.0% NaCl
3	1% NaCl	1.5% NaCl

(a) For each experiment, predict which way water will move.

_____ [1 mark]

(b) Water actually moved both into and out of the visking tubing in each experiment, explain why this happened.

_____

_____

_____ [3 marks]

B–A*

Osmosis and cells

1 Cells change shape when they are placed into solutions of different concentrations.

(a) Explain what happens to a plant cell when it is placed in a concentrated solution.

_____ [2 marks]

(b) Describe one similarity and one difference between what happens when you place an animal cell and a plant cell into pure water.

_____ [2 marks]

D–C

2 Sticks of the same-sized potato were placed into different sugar solutions and their change in size was measured.

(a) Explain why the potatoes have got bigger in the 0% sugar solution.

_____

_____

[2 marks]

(b) From the graph, identify the solution that is isotonic to the potatoes.

_____ [1 mark]

Graph: y-axis "Percentage change in the size of the potato" ranging from -1 to 0.6; x-axis "Percentage of sugar in the solution (M)" from 0 to 50.

B–A*

(c) Sports drinks are isotonic with human blood. List the components of sports drinks and why they are useful.

_____

_____

_____

_____ [6 marks]

Active transport

1 Active transport and diffusion are both forms of transport.

   (a) State two differences between diffusion and active transport.

     _____

     _____ [2 marks]

   (b) Predict with a reason, the time of day when the small intestine needs to use active transport rather than diffusion to absorb glucose.

     _____

     _____ [2 marks]

D–C

2 (a) Explain why root hair cells need to use active transport rather than diffusion to absorb minerals like nitrates from the soil.

     _____

     _____ [2 marks]

   (b) How are root hair cells adapted to use active transport?

     _____

     _____ [2 marks]

B–A*

Exchange surfaces

1 Exchange surfaces are needed in the body to absorb necessary molecules and to get rid of waste. Using the lungs as an example, answer the following questions

   (a) Where is the exchange surface in the lungs?

     _____ [1 mark]

   (b) What is exchanged in the lungs?

     _____

     _____ [2 marks]

D–C

2 Using your knowledge of villi, suggest how the structure of the lungs help in its exchange function.

     _____

     _____

     _____

     _____ [4 marks]

B–A*

Gas exchange

1 Gas exchange happens in the lungs, specifically in the alveoli.

   (a) Diffusion needs concentration gradients, state two ways that concentration gradients are maintained in the lungs.

     _____

     _____ [2 marks]

   (b) To be efficient, diffusion should occur over a short distance, give two ways the distance is kept short in the lungs.

     _____

     _____ [2 marks]

D–C

2 Scientists compared the lung to body size ratio of the lungs of various mammals, their results are in the graph.

   (a) Why are seal and whale lungs much bigger for their size than horse and human lungs?

     _____

     _____

     [2 marks]

   (b) Why would a horse need a bigger set of lungs for their size than humans?

     _____

     _____

     [2 marks]

   (c) Why would whales need a bigger set of lungs for their size than seals?

     _____

     _____ [2 marks]

Graph comparing the lung to body size ratio of some mammals

horse   human   seal   whale

B–A*

Breathing

1 Explain how air is taken into the lungs.

   _____

   _____

   _____

   _____

   _____ [5 marks]

D–C

2 Explain why monitoring the level of carbon dioxide in the blood can tell the brain when the body is low on oxygen.

   _____

   _____ [2 marks]

B–A*

Exchange in plants

1 Plants have adaptations for them to absorb the molecules and energy they need.

(a) Explain two adaptations leaves have to help in gas exchange.

_____ [2 marks]

(b) Explain why plants that grow under tall trees in rainforests have large flat leaves.

_____ [2 marks]

D–C

2 Explain how the cells in the leaf are adapted for maximum photosynthesis.

_____
_____
_____
_____ [4 marks]

B–A*

Transpiration

1 Three leaves of the same size were cut from a plant. The cut end of each leaf was sealed. The leaves were then covered in grease in different ways. All leaves were carefully weighed and placed in a window in a warm room. The results are given in the table.

	mass directly after greasing (g)	mass after six hours (g)
Leaf A (upper surface covered)	5	3
Leaf B (lower surface covered)	5	4.5
Leaf C (both surfaces covered)	6	6

(a) Using the results, suggest which surface is most important for water loss.

_____
_____ [2 marks]

(b) Why is leaf C heavier than the other leaves if they are all the same size?

_____ [1 mark]

(c) Name one way that you could increase the rate of transpiration and one way that you could decrease the rate of transpiration.

_____
_____ [2 marks]

D–C

2 Explain in detail how water is lost through transpiration.

_____
_____
_____ [4 marks]

B–A*

The circulatory system

1 Complete the table to show the functions of parts of the circulatory system.

Structure	Function
Left ventricle	
	carry blood away from the heart
Veins	
	the chamber that pumps blood to the lungs
Right atrium	

[5 marks]

D–C

2 Starting from the aorta list the vessels and the heart chambers that the blood travels through.

_____

_____

_____

_____ [4 marks]

B–A*

Blood vessels

1 The table shows the pressure in some blood vessels.

Blood vessel	Pressure (mmHg)
1	40
2	10
3	80
4	90

(a) Vessels 3 and 4 are both large arteries, suggest a reason for the difference in pressure.

_____

_____ [2 marks]

D–C

(b) What kind of vessels are 1 and 2, give a reason for your decision.

_____

_____ [2 marks]

2 Explain why veins need valves but arteries don't.

_____

_____

_____ [4 marks]

3 Explain how a diet of fatty foods can lead to heart disease, and include possible treatments.

_____

_____

_____

_____ [4 marks]

B–A*

Blood

1 Fill in the gaps in the following sentences.

Blood is mostly made of a pale liquid called _____. There are two types of cells, _____ which contain a red pigment called _____ and _____ which defend the body against harmful bacteria. There are also _____ which are needed for blood clotting.

[5 marks]

D–C

2 Name two nutrients, two gases and one waste product that the blood carries.

_____

_____

_____ [3 marks]

3 Explain how the small intestine, the kidney and the lungs affect what is in the blood.

B–A*

_____

_____

_____ [3 marks]

Transport in plants

1 Give two differences between phloem and xylem.

_____

_____ [2 marks]

2 For each condition given in the table, say whether transpiration would be faster or slower.

D–C

Condition	faster/slower
Moving a plant next to a fire	
Moving a plant away from a window into a corner	
Moving a plant inside a cupboard	
Moving a plant next to a fan	

[4 marks]

3 In transpiration osmosis, diffusion and pressure are all needed to move water, describe when each one is used.

B–A*

_____

_____

_____ [3 marks]

Waste and water control

1 List two waste products that the body makes, and the organs that help to get rid of them.

_____

_____ [2 marks]

2 Explain how kidneys balance the water concentration of the blood.

_____

_____

_____ [3 marks]

D–C

3 Scientists measured the concentration of urea in urine at different temperatures. The graph shows the results.

(a) What is the effect of temperature on the concentration of urea in urine?

_____ [1 mark]

(b) Explain the relationship between temperature and urine concentration.

_____

_____ [2 marks]

(c) Using the graph, predict the concentration of urea at 50 °C.

_____ [1 mark]

B–A*

Treating kidney disease

1 Discuss the advantages and disadvantages of both kidney dialysis and kidney transplants.

_____

_____

_____

_____ [4 marks]

D–C

2 Explain the causes, precautions and treatment for the rejection of donor kidneys.

_____

_____

_____

_____

_____ [5 marks]

B–A*

Temperature control

1 Fill in the gaps in the following sentences.

Temperature _____ on the skin send messages to the _____ in the brain when we become too _____ or too cold. The core body temperature should be _____.

[4 marks]

2 How could you tell by looking at someone if they were too hot? Give reasons.

_____

_____

_____

_____ [4 marks]

3 Explain what happens to the chemical reactions in our cells if we get too hot or too cold.

_____

_____ [2 marks]

Controlling blood glucose

1 Answer the following questions on blood glucose levels.

(a) What hormone is secreted when blood glucose rises too high?

_____ [1 mark]

(b) If someone's body can't respond to a change in glucose level, what disease do they have?

_____ [1 mark]

(c) What happens if blood glucose levels are too high?

_____

_____ [2 marks]

2 Fill in the flow chart to show what happens if blood glucose rises too high or drops too low.

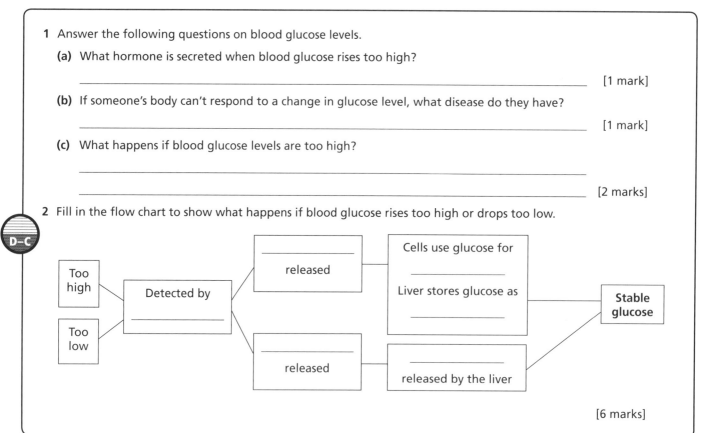

[6 marks]

Human waste

1 Give three reasons why there is less land available for wildlife.

field , building

quarrying , farming , building

[3 marks]

D–C

2 Give two different types of pollutants and describe how they affect the environment.

Water → pecide , sewege , fertiliser , toxic chemical

Air → CO_2 , SU_2 . smoke

land , pesticides + herbicides .

[4 marks]

3 Using an example, explain why making decisions about new developments is difficult.

Balance necessary progress with possible damage to environment .

B–A*

[3 marks]

Deforestation

1 Fill in the gaps in the following table about the consequences of deforestation.

Consequence	Reason
diversity	loss of habitat for wildlife
methane	growing of biofuels
increase in levels of methane in the atmosphere	rice field + cattle.
increase CO_2 , reduce amount of the. rate taken in.	the carbon locked in trees is burnt
more crops available	replace with crop

[6 marks]

D–C

① fuel .

2 Discuss the reasons for, and the consequences of, unsustainable harvesting of peat bogs.

Fe Extra CO_2 global warming/

② burning , increase CO_2

bacteria , active with oxygen ,

releau Ca

B–A*

[5 marks]

Global temperature

D–C

1 Give one advantage and one disadvantage of using biofuels.

_____

_____ [2 marks]

2 Give reasons for the following consequences of global warming:

  (a) rising sea levels _____

  (b) reduction in biodiversity _____

  (c) changes in migration patterns ___ migrate migrate, in wite
          (hot)

  (d) changes in species distribution ___ migrate for better condition ___ [4 marks]

B–A*

3 Explain the process of sequestering and how it can help reduce global warming.

_____

_____

_____

_____

_____

_____

_____ [6 marks]

Food production

D–C

1 List and explain two things that people can do to reduce the carbon emissions needed to produce their food.

___ ~~find~~ Justainable ___ △ vegetarian

___ Find replace resources ② eut local fuel ___ [2 marks]

___ reduce food mile

B–A*

2 Give advantages and disadvantages of cattle farmers limiting cows' movement and keeping them warm.

Ad: less respiration from movement and

heat, less energy lost, more efficient,

easy to control

___

___

Diə : not ethical

   e if there is disease ,

___ [4 marks]

Harvesting fish

1 Fish are being overfished in the oceans.

   (a) Describe three consequences of overfishing.

     smaller fish

     low fish stock.

     extinction.   **[3 marks]**   **D–C**

   (b) Describe two ways that we can prevent overfishing.

     restrict the net size.

     quota   **[2 marks]**

2 Explain why it is difficult to solve the problem of overfishing.

     need to make a living

     quota require international coor   **B–A***

     decide to g make quoty work,

     decide who to give which quots   **[4 marks]**

Fungus and mycoprotein

1 Give the steps needed to create mycoprotein in a fermenter.

     ① a oxygen, aerobic respiration.

     ②. fungus =>. Fusarium   **D–C**

     ③ glucose

     water bath => optimum T

     purified -> harvest   **[5 marks]**

2 Explain why mycoprotein is a more efficient form of protein than meat.

     ① made from plant, lower down food chain

     ② higher protein content   **B–A***

     ③ take less space than rearing cattle

     ④ waste from other   **[4 marks]**

Extended response question

Using at least two examples, explain the importance of active transport for living organisms and when it is used.

The quality of written communication will be assessed in your answer to this question.

_____

_____

_____

_____

_____

_____

_____

_____

_____

_____

_____

_____

_____

_____

_____

_____

_____

_____

_____

_____

_____

_____

_____

_____

_____

_____

_____

_____

_____

_____

_____

_____

_____

_____

_____

_____

_____

_____

_____

_____

_____

_____ [6 marks]

B1 Biology Checklist

1   I can describe how lifestyle can affect health ☐

2   I can explain how white blood cells defend us against pathogens ☐

3   I can describe how Semmelweiss reduced the number of deaths in hospitals and explain the key evidence that led him to his conclusions ☐

4   I can explain how vaccination produces immunity against a disease ☐

5   I can explain the limitations of antibiotics and the implications of their overuse ☐

6   I can describe how to safely grow cultures of microorganisms in the laboratory ☐

7   I can describe the pathway taken by a nerve impulse during a reflex action, including how the impulse crosses a junction between two neurones ☐

8   I can explain why it is important to keep temperature and blood sugar level constant ☐

9   I can describe how FSH, LH and oestrogen control the menstrual cycle ☐

10 I understand plant growth responses (tropisms) ☐

11 I can explain how drugs are tested in the laboratory and in clinical trials ☐

12 I can use the terms legal, illegal, dependency and addiction when discussing drugs ☐

13 I can describe adaptations of plants and animals and explain why they have these ☐

14 I can describe how energy is moved along a food chain ☐

15 I can describe what a pyramid of biomass shows us ☐

16 I can explain how carbon is constantly cycled ☐

17 I understand that different characteristics depend on different genes and the environment ☐

18 I can describe different cloning techniques ☐

19 I can describe the advantages and disadvantages of GM crops ☐

20 I can explain how natural selection works ☐

B2 Biology Checklist

1 I can describe the main features of animal, plant, bacterial and yeast cells ☐

2 I can describe the function of the different parts (organelles) of a cell ☐

3 I can describe how oxygen needed for respiration passes through cell membranes by diffusion ☐

4 I can explain that, in multicellular organisms, cells may differentiate and become specialised ☐

5 I can describe the function of a number of animal and plant tissues, organs and systems ☐

6 I can write down the word equation for photosynthesis ☐

7 I can describe the three factors that limit the rate of photosynthesis and how they affect the process ☐

8 I can list the range of substances, together with their uses, that plants can make from glucose ☐

9 I can describe how and why you would use quadrats and transects when investigating the distribution of organisms ☐

10 I can list some examples of the different types of protein found in the human body ☐

11 I can explain that enzymes act as catalysts, increasing the rate of chemical reactions ☐

12 I can describe at least one domestic and one industrial use of enzymes, including its advantages and disadvantages ☐

13 I can explain why anaerobic respiration releases less energy than aerobic respiration and results in an 'oxygen debt' ☐

14 I can explain what happens to chromosomes during mitosis and meiosis ☐

15 I can explain the inheritance of single characteristics by constructing genetic diagrams and using the terms homozygous, heterozygous, phenotype and genotype ☐

16 I can explain how different genes result in the production of different proteins ☐

17 I can describe the chromosome combinations that determine sex ☐

18 I can describe some of the ways in which fossils are formed ☐

19 I can give some of the reasons that organisms become extinct ☐

20 Explain the four key requirements in the formation of a new species ☐

B3 Biology Checklist

1   I understand that in osmosis water moves from a dilute solution to a concentrated solution ☑

2   I can describe how ions and water are lost in sweat ☐

3   I can explain that active transport goes against the concentration gradient ☐

4   I can recall two exchange surfaces and how they are adapted for diffusion ☐

5   I can describe how the ribs and diaphragm move in ventilation ☐

6   I can explain how roots and leaves are adapted for exchange ☐

7   I can describe the benefits and problems of transpiration ☐

8   I can describe the structure of the human heart ☐

9   I can describe the structure of arteries, veins and capillaries ☐

10 I can describe the function of the components of the blood ☐

11 I can describe the function of xylem and phloem ☐

12 I can recall where carbon dioxide and urea are removed from the body ☐

13 I can describe two treatments for kidney disease ☐

14 I can describe how body temperature is controlled ☐

15 I can describe the role of the pancreas in responding to changes in blood glucose ☐

16 I can describe how humans are polluting the Earth ☐

17 I can describe how biofuels and mycoprotein are made ☐

18 I can explain how concentration differences affect the movement of water across membranes ☐

19 I can explain the benefits of isotonic drinks ☐

20 I can explain how active transport occurs across membranes ☐

21 I can describe in detail how surface area to volume ratio increases the effectiveness of diffusion ☐

22 I can explain how inspiration and expiration are affected by pressure changes ☐

23 I can describe how the distribution of cells in the leaf aids in photosynthesis and gas exchange ☐

24 I can explain how environmental factors affect the rate of transpiration ☐

25 I can describe how stents are a treatment for blocked coronary arteries ☐

26 I can explain the role of haemoglobin in the transport of oxygen in the blood ☐

27 I can explain how water moves from the root into the xylem ☐

28 I can explain how the kidney filters urea from the blood and is involved in water balance ☐

29 I can compare the advantages and disadvantages of dialysis and transplants ☐

30 I can understand how the body controls its temperature ☐

31 I can describe how blood sugar is controlled and the consequences of diabetes ☐

32 I can explain how human activities are leading to global warming, deforestation and overfishing ☐

33 I can explain how biofuels and mycoprotein can help humans to be more sustainable ☐

Answers

B1 Answers

Pages 70–71

Diet and energy

1a Richard is exercising as well (more) [1]. Richard has a higher metabolic rate [1].

b If he exercises then he will use up stored fat to release energy [1]. If his metabolic rate is higher than Susan's, then chemical reactions in his cells will use up more energy than hers [1].

2 Fat releases double the amount of energy per gram compared to protein [1]. This energy gets stored as fat if it is not used up [1]. Proteins are used for growth and repair rather than energy [1].

Diet, exercise and health

1 A high level of cholesterol in the blood increases the risk of developing plaques [1] in the walls of the arteries that supply the heart with blood [1]. Plaques make it more likely that a blood clot will form in the artery. The clot can block the artery [1]. This will stop blood carrying oxygen getting to the heart muscle so the heart cells die [1]. This area of the heart no longer functions [1]. This is a heart attack.

2 HDL cholesterol helps to remove cholesterol from the walls of blood vessels [1]. So blood vessels are less likely to get blocked with blood clots and heart disease is less likely to develop. [1]

Pathogens and infections

1 Bacteria produce toxins [1]. Viruses reproduce inside our body cells [1]. When the cell gets filled up with viruses it bursts open, killing the cell [1].

2a Microorganisms are causing the infections [1] and the acid will kill them [1].

b The death rate to decrease. [1]

Fighting infection

1 By producing antibodies [1] and by producing antitoxins [1].

2a They can only attach themselves to one type of pathogen [1].

b Each lymphocyte produces one type of antibody [1]. Millions of different antibodies are needed so that most pathogens can be attacked and destroyed [1].

Pages 72–73

Drugs against disease

1a A drug that kills bacteria. [1]

b They spread the mucus onto a jelly [1] and add paper discs soaked in different antibiotics [1]. After a while they inspect the dish. The paper disc with the biggest clear area around it is the most effective antibiotic [1] because it stopped the growth of the bacteria in the mucus [1].

2 Overuse of antibiotics is making bacteria more resistant [1]. We need to reduce the amount of resistant bacteria, otherwise we will not be able to treat bacterial infections [1].

Antibiotic resistance

1 One bacteria in a person undergoes a random mutation which means it is resistant to an antibiotic [1]. The person takes antibiotics to kill the bacteria. It works, except for the resistant one [1]. The bacterium now has no competitors and grows rapidly [1]. It divides and makes lots of identical copies of itself [1]. There is now a population of antibiotic-resistant bacteria.

2 Deaths rose between 1993 and 2006 [1], and decreased between 2006 and 2008 [1]. They rose because MRSA was multiplying rapidly and nothing was put in place to stop this [1]. After 2006, people became more aware of the threat of MRSA and started putting in preventative measures, especially in hospitals, e.g. staff washing hands more thoroughly, hospital wards kept cleaner, visitors cleaning hands on entrance to hospital [1].

Vaccination

1a It is to stop children getting measles, mumps and rubella. [1]

b A small amount of the dead or inactive viruses that cause the diseases is injected into the blood [1]. The white blood cells attack them, just as they would attack living pathogens [1]. They remember how to make the antibody [1], so the child is now immune to the diseases.

c There was a study published that linked the vaccine to autism. [1]

d It was discovered that there was never any evidence to prove the link. [1]

2 The flu is a new type that has formed from the virus mutating [1]. A new vaccine has been developed, as the old vaccine would not be effective against the new virus [1].

Growing bacteria

1 If it was 37 °C or more, it would encourage the growth of pathogens that live in the body [1]. If the dish is then opened, the pathogens could escape and cause illness [1].

2 This temperature will promote rapid growth [1], which will make the product that you are culturing available quickly and so maximise profits [1].

Pages 74–75

Co-ordination, nerves and hormones

1 The brain and spinal cord. [1]

2a The heart responds to adrenalin. [1]

b It is longer lasting [1] so the response [increased heart rate] is maintained throughout the tennis match [1].

Receptors

1a sensory [1]

b arrow drawn to the right [1]

c (electrical) impulses [1]

2a cones [1]

b Impulses [1] from several cones [1] travel along the optic nerve [1] to the brain.

Reflex actions

1 Receptors in the skin detect the pin/pain [1], impulse sent along sensory neurone to spinal cord [1], impulse travels across synapse to relay neurone [1], impulse travels across synapse to motor neurone [1], impulse travels along motor neurone to arm muscle [1], muscle contracts pulling hand away [1].

2a conscious [1]

b Falling over is more dangerous than touching the hot radiator. [1]

Controlling the body

1 This is the temperature that enzymes work best at [1]. Without enzymes, important chemical reactions in the body would not take place [1].

2 Exertion will cause your body temperature to rise [1], and you will sweat to bring it back down to normal [1]. This will cause a loss of water [1]. A low water concentration in the body is dangerous because cells will stop working [1].

Pages 76–77

Reproductive hormones

1 High levels of oestrogen stop the production of FSH [1]. Without FSH, eggs cannot mature [1] so no eggs are released to be fertilised [1].

2 Low oestrogen levels between days 0–4 cause the uterus lining to break down and menstruation to occur [1]. A rise between days 4–14 makes the lining build up again [1]. A decrease around day 13 triggers ovulation [1].

Controlling fertility

1 Fertility drugs are given to stimulate the maturation of several eggs [1]. Eggs are collected and fertilised by sperm from the father [1]. The embryos formed are inserted into the mother's uterus (womb) [1].

2a Fertility drugs increase the amount of eggs released at a time [1], so it's more likely that three get fertilised [1].

b Triplets are more likely to have problems developing in the uterus than a single fetus [1] but medical treatment has improved in the last century so more survive [1].

Plant responses and hormones

1a positive [1]

b negative [1]

2a Cover or remove the tip of the seedling [1]. Use a control that has had no treatment [1]. Grow both in the presence of light coming from one direction [1].

b The plant with no tip does not grow towards the light (straight up) [1]. The shoot of the control plant does grow towards the light [1].

Drugs

1 i One mark for any legal drug: e.g. alcohol or nicotine.

ii One mark for any illegal drug: e.g. cannabis or heroin.

b Nicotine is addictive [1], so a person will suffer withdrawal symptoms if they stop smoking [1].

2 Any two reasons from, for example: liver failure [1], car accident [1], alcohol poisoning [1].

Pages 78–79

Developing new drugs

1a Some of the volunteers are given a placebo [1], which does not contain the drug [1], but neither they nor their doctor knows whether they have been given it [1].

b the age of the soldiers [1]

c One reason, for example: the recovery time for the soldiers who took the drug was less than for those who took the placebo. [1]

2 They only tested the drug on one group of people [1], so these people may not have been predisposed to develop the side-effects that were seen when the general population started taking the drug [1]. The trial did not last very long [1], and the side-effects are only seen when the person has been taking the drug for several months or years [1].

Legal and illegal drugs

1a The number of deaths from drinking alcohol has risen (between the years 2000 and 2008) [1]. More men die from drinking alcohol then women [1].

b The number of people who died from alcohol is much higher than those who died from heroin (9031, which is around 10 times higher) [1]. This is because many more people drink alcohol than take heroin [1].

2 They give them an unfair advantage over their competitors (they could be banned from the sport) [1]. They could cause long-lasting damage [1].

Competition

1 The weeds will compete with the vegetable plants (for light, water, space and nutrients) [1], so the vegetable plants will not be able to grow as well [1].

2 They do not have to compete for resources [1] so are more likely to get what they need to survive [1] and breed [1].

Adaptations for survival

1a It deters predators from eating it. [1]

b The yellow and black are warning colours [1] so predators of the hoverfly think it is dangerous and leave it alone [1].

2 Extremophiles can survive in very difficult environments [1] so microorganisms could survive on Mars where conditions are difficult [1].

Pages 80–81

Environmental change

1 Numbers will decrease [1] because plants will die through lack of water [1] so there will be less food for them [1].

2a Food prices will increase.

b With fewer honeybees, fewer plants will be pollinated [1] so less food crops will develop [1].

Pollution indicators

1a oxygen meter [1]

b It is low. [1]

c Mayfly larvae / freshwater shrimp / stonefly larva [1]. They can only live in unpolluted water [1].

2 They can maximise the uptake of oxygen [1] from polluted water where oxygen is low [1].

Food chains and energy flow

1 One reason from: some of the light misses the leaves altogether / hits the leaf and reflects / hits the leaf but goes all the way through without hitting any chlorophyll / hits the chlorophyll but is not absorbed because it is of the wrong wavelength (colour). [1]

2a 800 × (10/100) = 80 units

b To increase the chance of capturing light [1] so they can photosynthesise more efficiently [1].

Biomass

1 The sketch should show: a pyramid with the levels labelled with the name of the organism, starting with

   grass at the bottom [1], each level should then get progressively smaller [1].

2 Most animals in the ocean are cold-blooded so they do not use energy to regulate their temperature [1]. This means that less energy is lost from the food chain at each stage [1], so energy can be passed along to more organisms [1].

Pages 82–83

Decay

1a To increase the moisture content [1] so the numbers of microorganisms in the compost increase [1], which speeds up decay and the production of compost [1].

b To let in oxygen [1] so the microorganisms responsible for decay can live (respire) [1].

c It contains nutrients [1] that increase their growth [1].

2 The high temperatures kill any microorganisms in the food [1], the sealing prevents any more from entering [1] so decay cannot happen [1].

Recycling

1 Added to food chain diagram: a label saying 'microorganisms' [1], with arrows from all grass, antelope and lion pointing towards it [1].

2 Scavengers eat the bodies of dead animals [1]. Microorganisms break down waste and dead bodies and release the nutrients (decay) [1].

The carbon cycle

1a i combustion/burning [1]

   ii photosynthesis [1]

b from eating plants or other animals [1]

c The animal will die [1] and the tissue will be decayed by microorganisms [1] which will carry out respiration [1] and release carbon dioxide [1].

2a i light → chemical [2]

   ii chemical → heat and light (and sound) [2]

b The chemical energy in food is released during respiration [1] and transferred to movement energy in the muscles of an animal [1].

Genes and chromosomes

1 He inherited one from his mother in her egg [1] and one from his father in his sperm [1].

2a Bush A: 66.7 cm [1]; Bush B: 71.9 cm [1].

b To improve the reliability of her results. [1]

c Bushes have each inherited a different gene for leaf length [1]. Environment will also be a factor as the bushes will each receive different amounts of water/light [1].

Pages 84–85

Reproduction

1a asexual [1]

b It has the same genes. [1]

c They reproduce sexually [1] so have a different mix of genes [1].

2a In internal fertilisation, the egg and the sperm meet inside the female's body [1]. In external fertilisation, they meet outside of the female's body [1].

b To increase the chance of fertilisation [1] so at least a few offspring develop [1].

Cloning plants and animals

1a So she has many identical copies of it. [1]

b Either: use tissue culture [1], take a piece of the tissue from the plant [1] and grow it in a sterile nutrient liquid or gel [1].
   Or: take a cutting [1], cut off a small piece of the stem [1] dip it in hormone rooting powder and place it in soil [1].

2a To produce lots of animals so it is no longer extinct. [1]

b Take eggs from a goat of a similar species and remove the nucleus [1], then take a preserved cell from the ibex and remove the nucleus [1]. Insert the nucleus from the ibex cell into the egg [1], then put the formed embryo into a donor mother goat [1].

Genetic engineering

1a They have genes from another organism.

b The gene for insulin is cut from a human chromosome; and a chromosome from bacterium is cut open using enzymes [1]. The insulin gene is inserted into the bacterium's chromosome [1]. The chromosome is put back into the bacterium [1].

c The bacteria grow best at this temperature [1] so insulin is produced more quickly [1].

2a They will not have to use pesticides [1], will get higher yields of cotton as less are destroyed by pests [1] and make more profit [1].

b Any sensible answer, for example: The toxins may affect other wildlife / disrupt food chains / the Bt gene may be transferred to other plants.

Evolution

1 Giraffes will have a gene for long necks [1] which would be passed on to their offspring [1]; and reaching for leaves cannot change the gene [1].

2 For: We have evidence that all life on Earth, including complex organisms such as humans, evolved from simple single-celled organisms [1].

Against: There are millions of species of bacteria on Earth [1] that are adapted to their environment and so will not evolve [1].

Page 86
Natural selection

1a It's the same colour as the tree trunk (camouflaged) [1]. Makes it difficult to be spotted by predators [1].

b a change in a gene [1]

c The black moths are now camouflaged [1], so they do not get eaten [1] and they live to reproduce and pass on the gene to their offspring [1].

2 The resistance is caused by a mutation [1] which happens by chance [1]. A rat that has a mutation survives, and passes it on to its offspring [1].

Evidence for evolution

1a Because each animal uses its limbs differently/they are adapted [1].

b They all have the bones in the same place [1] which shows that birds, bats and humans all have a common ancestor [1] from which they evolved [1].

2a Archaea [1] because they are closer on the tree [1].

b A common ancestor [1] from which all life on Earth evolved [1].

Page 87
Extended response question
5–6 marks

A detailed description of how a difference in concentration of auxins in the developing root will cause the roots to bend downwards. The answer will include information such as that in the roots a high concentration of auxins inhibits cell elongation. Auxin tends to accumulate on the lower side of a root. The lower side of the shoot grows more slowly than the upper surface. This causes the root to bend downwards. This is a tropism called gravitropism (or geotropism).

All information in answer is relevant, clear, organised and presented in a structured and coherent format. Specialist terms are used appropriately. Few, if any, errors in grammar, punctuation and spelling.

3–4 marks

Limited description of why a root bends downwards. The answer will state that auxins inhibit cell growth in roots. The upper side of the root will grow more, causing it to bend and this causes the root to bend downwards.

For the most part the information is relevant and presented in a structured and coherent format. Specialist terms are used for the most part appropriately. There are occasional errors in grammar, punctuation and spelling.

1–2 marks

An incomplete description, stating that the upper side of the root will grow more, causing it to bend downwards.

Answer may be simplistic. There may be limited use of specialist terms. Errors of grammar, punctuation and spelling prevent communication of the science.

B2 Answers

Pages 88–89

Animal and plant cells

1a plant [1]

b A: cell wall [1] B: vacuole [1]

c It's where protein synthesis takes place. [1]

d Chloroplasts absorb light energy to make food [photosynthesis] [1]. Roots are underground where there is no light so have no need for chloroplasts [1]. Leaf cells do receive light so require many chloroplasts [for photosynthesis] [1].

2 Viruses are very small [1] so need to be magnified many times in order to be studied [1]. Electron microscopes can magnify objects more than a light microscope [1].

Microbial cells

1a Similarity: Both have cell wall / nucleus / cytoplasm / cell membrane / vacuole / ribosomes. [1]
Difference: Plant cell wall is made of cellulose, yeast cell wall isn't / Yeast does not contain chloroplasts. [1]

b Similarity: Both have cytoplasm/cell membrane. [1]
Difference: Animal cell has a nucleus. Bacteria do not / Bacteria has a cell wall. Animal cells do not. [1]

2 20/0.02 = 1000 [1 mark]

Diffusion

1 The scent of the cake is caused by cake molecules [1]. The concentration of cake molecules will be high in the kitchen [1] but low in other parts of the house [1]. There will be a net movement of molecules from where there is a high concentration to a lower one [1] so the cake molecules will spread away from the kitchen into the rest of the house.

2a They use it up [for respiration]. [1]

b So the concentration remains higher in the blood [1] and therefore glucose keeps on diffusing into the cells [1].

c There will be glucose inside the visking tubing [1] because glucose has diffused across the membrane of the tubing [1] from where it is in a high concentration to a lower one [1].

Specialised cells

1 It has haemoglobin [1] to transport oxygen [1] /a disc shape [1] for taking in and letting out oxygen [1].

2 It has a 'hair' protruding from the cell [1], which increases the surface area [1] to increase water absorption [1].

Pages 90–91

Tissues

1a muscle [1]

b to release energy [1] which the cells need to contract [1]

2a diffusion [1]

b They increase the surface area of the lungs. [1]

c Bacteria are just one cell [1] whereas humans are many cells, so the oxygen has to be transported around the body so all cells are supplied with oxygen [1].

Animal tissues and organs

1 One mark for each: 1A, 2D, 3E, 4B, 5C.

2 They protect the intestinal cells [1] from being digested by the juices that get mixed with the food [1]. By producing mucus which adds a barrier [1] this also makes it easier for the food to slide through the digestive system [1].

Plant tissues and organs

1a i It stops too much water leaving the leaf [1] and protects the underlying cells [1].

ii to carry out photosynthesis [1]

b xylem [1]

2a They allow gases to diffuse into and out of the leaf. [1]

b To stop too much water escaping from the leaf. [1]

Photosynthesis

1a The leaves will not go black. [1]

b No starch was present [1] because the plants were in the dark so could not carry out photosynthesis [1] so no glucose was made which is stored as starch [1].

c The part that went black was green [1] and had carried out photosynthesis to produce starch [1] because the cells contain chlorophyll [1]. The bits that stayed orange were white so did not carry out photosynthesis and produce starch [1].

2 It absorbs the red and blue part of white light [1] which are needed to drive photosynthesis [1] and reflects the green part [1].

Pages 92–93

Limiting factors

1a oxygen [1]

b As the light intensity increases, the rate of photosynthesis increases. [1]

c The rate of photosynthesis stops increasing. [1]

d Another factor is limiting the rate of photosynthesis, e.g. concentration of carbon dioxide [1] so even if the light intensity increases the rate of photosynthesis cannot [1].

2a Any sensible suggestion, for example: the plants would be taller / the tomatoes would be bigger / the tomatoes would taste sweeter. [1]

b The heater increases the temperature [1], and the automatic watering system ensures that plants always have water [1].

c a source [increased concentration] of carbon dioxide [1]

The products of photosynthesis

1 It adds nitrogen to glucose [1]. Nitrogen comes from nitrate ions [1] which are absorbed from the soil through the roots [1].

2a for the plant embryo to grow [1]

b Oil contains a high amount of energy per gram [1] so the seed is light and can be easily dispersed by the wind [1].

Distribution of organisms

1a There's not enough light [1] so plants cannot photosynthesise [1].

b It needs to be where it will be covered in water for some periods of the day [1] or it will get too hot and dry out [1].

2a The distribution of the grey squirrel has increased and the distribution of the red squirrel has decreased. [1]

b There is competition between the grey and red squirrels for food [1]. The grey squirrels are better adapted so will win [1], they will survive while the red squirrels will die [1].

Using quadrats to sample organisms

1a 4×8 [1 mark] = 32 [1 mark]

b Make sure that the quadrat is placed randomly. [1]

2 This size contained a reasonably high number of different species inside (fifteen) [1]. A larger quadrat would have contained more [1] but it would have made it more difficult for her to count the number of species inside it [1].

Pages 94–95

Proteins

1a amino acids [1]

b The order determines the shape of the protein [1]. The protein will only function correctly if the shape is right [1].

2 Protein in food gets broken down by enzymes [1] into amino acids [1], which are transported to leg muscle cells in the blood [1]. Muscle protein is made on ribosomes [1] using instructions from genes [1].

Enzymes

1a i starch [1]

ii sugars [1]

b temperature [1]

c Any one from: concentration of starch/amylase, volume of starch/amylase, room temperature. [1]

2 Between 0 °C and 40 °C, the rate of reaction increased [1] because the molecules of starch and amylase had increasing amounts of energy [1] and were colliding more frequently and with more energy so they reacted to break down the starch more often [1]. After 40 °C, the rate started to slow down [1] as the amylase started to change shape [denature] [1] so the starch no longer fitted into the active site so the reaction could not occur [1].

Enzymes and digestion

1a starch [1]

b salivary [1]

c protease [1]

d stomach [1]

e lipase [1]

f glycerol [1]

2a 7.5 [1]

b i so as to provide the optimum pH for the enzyme pepsin [1]

ii Bile [1] mixes with the food which is alkaline [1] and neutralises the acid [1].

Enzymes at home

1a It contains lipase [1] which will break down the fat [1] so it becomes soluble and washes away [1].

b The stain will not come out [1] because the lipase will not work at this temperature [1]. It will denature [1].

2a To a test tube of egg white, add some biological detergent [1]. To another test tube of egg white, add the same volume of distilled water [1]. Leave both in a water bath at 30 °C [1]. If the egg white has dissolved (gone clear), the detergent has broken it down [1].

b She is not using keratin. [1]

Pages 96–97

Enzymes in industry

1a by using carbohydrase enzymes [1]

b Starch solution is cheaper. [1]

c Fructose is sweeter than glucose [1] so less is needed [1], which lowers the energy [calorie] content of the food [1].

d isomerase [1]

2a fructose [1] and glucose [1]

b making soft-centre chocolates [1]

Aerobic respiration

1a For respiration [1], to release energy from glucose [1].

b Air enters the lungs [1] and oxygen travels into the blood [1].

2 Carbon dioxide is low at 6 a.m. and 6 p.m. because it is dark and the plant is not carrying out photosynthesis [1], so the leaves do not absorb carbon dioxide [1]. It is highest at 12 p.m. because this is the brightest part of the day and the rate of photosynthesis is at a maximum [1].
Oxygen uptake is lowest at 12 p.m. because the plant is using oxygen produced from photosynthesis [1] for respiration [1] [there is no need for it to absorb any from the air]. Oxygen is high at 6 a.m. and 6 p.m. because the plant is only carrying out respiration and so needs to absorb oxygen from the air [1].

Using energy

1a His muscles are contracting [1] and using up energy [1].

b His body will use up more energy [1] to maintain his body temperature [1].

2 The muscle has to contract at all times [1] so needs a large supply of energy [1]. Mitochondria are where energy is made via respiration [1].

Anaerobic respiration

1a Aerobic respiration releases more energy per gram of glucose [1], anaerobic produces lactic acid which is toxic [1].

b She is taking in extra oxygen [1] to break down the lactic acid that has formed in her muscles [1].

2a So he is fitter [can swim faster and for longer without getting tired]. [1]

b cross-country skiing [1]

c His heart and lungs will get stronger [1] and more efficient at getting oxygen to his muscles [1], so he can respire more efficiently [1] and swim faster and for longer.

Pages 98–99

Cell division – mitosis

1a The parent cell divides into two. [1]

b They have the same chromosomes. [1]

c To replace old skin cells that die/to repair cuts in the skin. [1]

2a A copy of each has been made. [1]

b The copies of chromosomes are being pulled apart [1] to form two cells with the same chromosomes [1].

Cell division – meiosis

1a ovaries [1]

b Cells: 1 = 64 [1], 2 and 3 = 64 [1], 4, 5, 6 and 7 = 32 [1]

c It forms gametes with half the normal number of chromosomes [1], so during fertilisation a zygote is formed with a full set of chromosomes [1].

2 Any four from: Mitosis forms new body cells and meiosis forms gametes [1]. Mitosis happens in all parts of the body and meiosis only happens in the testes and ovaries [1]. In mitosis the cell divides once but in meiosis there are two cell divisions [1]. In mitosis two cells are made and in meiosis four are made [1]. In mitosis the new cells have the same number of chromosomes as the original cell. In meiosis the new cells have half the number of chromosomes as the original cell. [1]

Stem cells

1 Stem cells could be taken from an embryo or adult bone marrow [1] and placed into the brain of the patient [1] where they differentiate to form new brain cells [1].

2 Any 3 points from: Their practice is probably unregulated and so potentially dangerous or will not work [1]/they may use embryonic stem cells which some people find morally wrong [1]/the stem cells may be rejected [1]/the stem cells they use may carry genetic mutations for disease [1]/the treatment may trigger side-effects [1].

Genes, alleles and DNA

1a possible father B [1]

b The child shares DNA fragments with him [1] which were transferred from the father in his sperm [1].

2a People who carry the BRCA mutation are more likely to develop breast cancer than the general population [1]. The older you get, the higher the chance of developing breast cancer [1].

b She may have inherited the BRCA mutation [1] which increases her risk of developing breast cancer [1].

Pages 100–101

Mendel

1 His ideas were only accepted when scientists had discovered how characteristics were inherited [genes/chromosomes]. [1]

2a The offspring would all be medium height. [1]

b The tallness allele was dominant over the shortness allele [1]. All the offspring have one tallness allele and one shortness allele [1] so they are all tall [1].

How genes affect characteristics

1a One from each parent. [1]

b bb [1]

c In either order [but always a capital letter first]: Bb [1] BB [1].

2 The Y chromosome [1] because only males have it [1].

Inheriting chromosomes and genes

1a The one for short hair. [1]

b Hh [accept any letter as long as there is an upper case and corresponding lower case] [1]

c

Parent	short-haired	long-haired	
	Hh	hh	[1]
Gametes	H and h	h and h	[1]
Offspring		H	h

	H	h
h	Hh	hh
h	Hh	hh

[1 mark]

d 1:1 [1 mark]

2 He could breed the green-seeded plant with a yellow-seeded one [1]. If all of the offspring are green then the genotype is most likely to be homozygous dominant [GG] [1]. If some of the offspring are yellow then it is most likely to be heterozygous [Gg] [1].

How genes work

1 The allele is a section of DNA [1]. The order of the bases in the DNA is a code [1] to make a brown protein [pigment] [1] that the cells in her eye produce [1].

2 Joshua could have a mutation in the insulin gene [1], which means that the DNA no longer codes for, and so does not produce, insulin [1].

Pages 102–103

Genetic disorders

1a cc [or any answer with two lower-case letters] [1]

b Their child [E] has cystic fibrosis [1] so they must have each passed on the cystic fibrosis allele [1].

c 50 per cent/1 in 2 [1]

2 Use IVF to produce several embryos [1]. Check the DNA of the embryos [1]. Only implant the embryo[s] free of the alleles that cause the disease into Louise's uterus. [1]

Fossils

1 There are not many fossils of jellyfish [1] as they just decay [1], so scientists do not have a lot of evidence of how they used to look millions of years ago [1].

2a All life on Earth uses the same genetic code. [1]

b Valid and reliable evidence [1]. Agreement between most scientists [1].

Extinction

1 Any two from: The trout are eating them/The trout are better adapted at catching food/The trout are carrying a disease which they pass onto the fish. [2]

2a High numbers of species become extinct [1] over a short period of time [1].

b A higher number of fossils have been found dating from that time. [1]

c The small mammals were better adapted [1] to living at the colder temperatures [1] than the dinosaurs.

New species

1 On each island there is a different environment [1]. The finches show variation [1] and the ones better adapted to living on that island survive [1] to pass on these genes to their offspring [1]. The finches on each island change so much from the mainland species that they are a new species [1].

2 It can no longer breed with the other grass [1] because to breed together the flowers have to form at the same time [1]. As they can no longer breed, they are separate species [1].

Page 104

Extended response question

5-6 marks

A detailed description of how prolonged exposure to temperatures above 37 °C results in the denaturation of enzymes and how this effects their ability to function. The answer should contain details about the importance of the shape of the enzyme and why the functioning of enzymes is vital for life. All information in answer is relevant, clear, organised and presented in a structured and coherent format. Specialist terms are used appropriately. Few, if any, errors in grammar, punctuation and spelling.

3-4 marks

Limited description of how high temperatures affect enzymes. The answer will state that temperatures over 37 °C leads to a change in shape of the enzyme which inhibits its function. For the most part the information is relevant and presented in a structured and coherent format. Specialist terms are used for the most part appropriately. There are occasional errors in grammar, punctuation and spelling.

1-2 marks

An incomplete description, stating that enzymes do not work over 37 °C. Answer may be simplistic. There may be limited use of specialist terms. Errors of grammar, punctuation and spelling prevent communication of the science.

B3 Answers

Page 105

Osmosis

1a Visking tubing is partially permeable. [1]

b a partially permeable membrane [1] and a concentration gradient/two different concentrations [1]

2a 1 – into the beaker; 2 – no net movement; 3 – into the visking tubing (1 mark for three correct answers)

b Osmosis happens because of the random movement of water molecules [1]; overall the water will move towards the concentrated solution [1] but if water molecules in the concentrated solution randomly hit the holes in the visking tubing they will move into the more dilute solution [1].

Osmosis and cells

1a Water leaves the cell by osmosis because of the concentration gradient [1], the plasma membrane pulls away from the cell wall [1].

b Similarity: in both, the water moves into the cell by osmosis [1].
Difference: the animal cell bursts but the plant cell gets bigger [1].

2a The surroundings are more dilute than the cytoplasm [1], water moves into the cells and they get bigger [1].

b 15%

c water [1] rehydrates cells [1]; ions [1] keeps water balance [1]; sugar [1] replaces sugar used in respiration [1]

Pages 106–107

Active transport

1a Active transport needs energy, diffusion doesn't [1], active transport goes against the concentration gradient, diffusion goes along it [1].

b Just before breakfast/early morning [1], as there isn't much food in the intestine after sleeping [1].

2a The concentration of nitrates is lower than in the cytoplasm [1], so nitrates are absorbed against their concentration gradient [1].

b They have lots of mitochondria [1] so there is energy for active transport [1] [don't accept large surface area as this is more important for diffusion].

Exchange surfaces

1a alveoli [1]

b Oxygen into the blood [1], carbon dioxide into the air [1].

2 Having lots of alveoli [1] increases surface area [1]; a dense network of capillaries [1] maintains concentration gradient [1]; or alveoli made of flattened cells one cell thick [1] makes for a short distance for diffusion [1].

Gas exchange

1a Blood is moved through capillaries [1], ventilation exchanges the air [1].

b Capillaries and alveoli are one cell thick [1]/made of flattened cells [1].

2a They are aquatic and spend a lot of time under water [1] so when they are on land they need to breath in as much oxygen as possible [1].

b Horses are larger/move faster than humans [1] and so need more oxygen for respiration [1].

c Whales stay underwater for much longer than seals [1] so they need a larger surface area when they do rise for air [1].

Breathing

1 The diaphragm contracts [1], one set of intercostal muscles contracts [1], muscle contraction increases the volume in the thorax [1] and this lowers the pressure [1], sucking air into the lungs [1].

2 Carbon dioxide is produced by respiration [1] more oxygen is needed when lots of respiration is happening e.g. during exercise [1].

Pages 108–109

Exchange in plants

1a Stomata to allow gas exchange [1], thin leaves for a short diffusion distance [1].

b light is blocked by the trees [1] so large flat leaves can trap as much light as possible [1]

2 The top layer of cells are closely packed together [1] to trap the maximum amount of light [1], cells in the middle layer have air spaces [1] to allow the diffusion of carbon dioxide and oxygen [1].

Transpiration

1a Lower surface [1] because when it is covered there is a smaller mass decrease [1].

b There are two layers of grease and the others only have one [1].

c Increase – have a fan/breeze blowing on the leaves [1]; decrease – move the leaves into a colder room [1]

2 Water moves from the inside of the cell across the membrane [1], it evaporates from the cell wall [1], the vapour then moves through the air spaces [1] it then diffuses out of the stomata [1].

The circulatory system

1

Structure	Function
Left ventricle	*the chamber that pumps blood to the body*
Arteries	carry blood away from the heart
Veins	*carry blood to the heart*
Right ventricle	the chamber that pumps blood to the lungs
Right atrium	*the chamber that collects blood from the body*

2 aorta → (body) → vena cava → right atrium → right ventricle → pulmonary artery → (lungs) → pulmonary vein → left atrium → left ventricle → [back to the aorta] [give one mark for every 2 that are correct] [4]

Blood vessels

1a Vessel 4 is the aorta and 3 is the pulmonary artery [1], blood is pumped at a higher pressure from the left ventricle [1].

b Vessel 2 is a vein because it has the lowest pressure [1], vessel 1 is a capillary because it's pressure is lower than the artery and higher than the vein/in the middle [1].

2 Arteries have high pressure [1] so blood cannot flow backwards [1], veins are at low pressure/(and) returning to the heart [1] so valves are needed as there is more risk of blood flowing backwards [1].

3 Fatty foods contain cholesterol [1], cholesterol forms plaques [1] in coronary arteries [1], a stent can keep the coronary arteries open [1].

Pages 110–111

Blood

1 plasma [1], red blood cells [1], haemoglobin [1], white blood cells [1], platelets [1]

2 nutrients – glucose, amino acids [1]; gases – oxygen, carbon dioxide [1]; waste – urea [1]

3 In the small intestine, nutrients enter the blood [1]; the kidneys extract urea and excess water [1]; in the lungs carbon dioxide exits and oxygen enters the blood [1].

Transport in plants

1 Phloem carries dissolved sugar, xylem carries water and minerals [1]; phloem are alive and xylem are dead [1]; phloem can move down (and up) and xylem can only move up [1].

2 faster [1]; slower [1]; slower [1]; faster [1]

3 Osmosis is used when water enters the roots [1]; water moves from an area of high pressure to an area of low pressure in the stem/xylem [1]; water diffuses out of the stomata [1].

Waste and water control

1 carbon dioxide, the lungs [1]; and urea, the kidney [1]

2 Water is absorbed into the kidney [1]; some of it is reabsorbed [1], excess water is used to make urine [1].

3a As temperature increases, the concentration of urea increases/there is a positive correlation [1].

b As the temperature increases we lose more water in sweat [1], so there is less excess water [1].

c around 8.8 ± 0.2 °C

Treating kidney disease

1 Advantages: dialysis – widely available [1]; transplant – can live a normal life afterwards [1]
Disadvantages: dialysis – takes a long time every week/larger risk of illness [1]; transplant – risk of rejection/limited number of kidneys [1]

2 Causes – donor kidneys have foreign antigens [1]; the body thinks these could be harmful so attacks them [1].
Precautions – donor and recipient are matched as closely as possible [1], living relatives are used if they are a match [1].
Treatment – immunosuppressant drugs are needed for the rest of their lives [1].

Page 112–113

Temperature control

1 sensors [1]; thermoregulatory region [1]; hot [1]; 37 °C [1]

2 Their skin would be pink [1] because skin arterioles dilate [1]; they would be sweating [1] because evaporation uses heat energy from the skin to cool us down [1].

3 Too hot – reactions go faster/then stop [1]; too cold – reactions go slower [1].

Controlling blood glucose

1a insulin

b diabetes

c Water is drawn out of cells by osmosis [1], which can lead to permanent damage [1].

2 Too high – pancreas [1]; insulin [1]; respiration [1]; glycogen [1].
Too low – pancreas [1]; glucagon [1]; glycogen [1].

Human waste

1 quarrying [1]; building [1]; farming [1]

2 Sulfur dioxide [1] leads to acid rain [1] / pesticides [1] kill wildlife / herbicides [1] kill wildlife / sewage [1] kills aquatic animals [1] (accept any two pairs of type and effect)

3 You have to balance necessary progress with possible damage to the environment [1] e.g., a toll road destroys habitat/leads to more journeys [1] but may result in less pollution from traffic jams [1].

Deforestation

1

Consequence	Reason
decrease in biodiversity	loss of habitat for wildlife
reduces dependency on oil	growing of biofuels
increase in levels of methane in the atmosphere	cattle and rice paddies replace forests
increase in carbon dioxide in the atmosphere	the carbon locked in trees is burnt
	a decrease in photosynthesis which captures carbon
more crops available	forests are replaced with crops

2 Peat bogs are harvested for fuel/improving soil [1]; consequences – increase in carbon dioxide [1] from burning of peat [1], bacteria becoming active with increased oxygen [1] releasing carbon dioxide in respiration [1].

Pages 114–115

Global temperature

1 Advantage – has lower carbon emissions [1]; disadvantage – takes land away from crops/wildlife [1].

2a As temperature rises ice caps melt / water expands. [1]

b If climate changes, some species won't be able to adapt and may become extinct. [1]

c Some animals may not migrate for the winter. [1]

d Species may migrate to find a better climate. [1]

3 Carbon dioxide dissolves in the water [1], some shellfish use carbon to make cells [1] and algae use it for photosynthesis [1], animals eat algae [1], dead organisms containing carbon fall to the bottom of the ocean [1], some dead organisms become part of limestone [1].

Food production

1 Be a vegetarian/eat less meat, as the lower the stage in the food chain the greater the efficiency [1]; eat locally, as local food has lower food miles [1].

2 Limiting movement
Advantage – makes the farming more efficient/ because more food is converted to muscle [1].
Disadvantage – stops cows living a natural life/cruel to the cows [1].

Keeping animals warm
Advantage – makes the farming more efficient/more food is converted to muscle/animals don't feel discomfort from being cold [1].

Disadvantage – stops cows from living a natural life [1].

Harvesting fish

1a smaller fish [1]; low fish stocks [1]; extinction [1]

b banning nets with small holes [1]; imposing quotas [1]

2 Fisherman don't want to reduce their catches because they need to make a living [1]; quotas require international cooperation [1]; it is difficult to regulate quotas [1]; it is difficult to decide who gets which quota [1].

Fungus and mycoprotein

1 Glucose is added to feed Fusarium [1], an optimum temperature is maintained through a water bath [1], air is bubbled through [1] to mix and add oxygen for aerobic conditions [1], then fungus is harvested/ purified and shaped [1].

2 It is lower down the food chain [1], it has a higher protein content than the same mass of meat [1]; it takes up less space than rearing cattle [1], it can use waste from other processes as a food source [1].

Page 116

Extended Response Question

5–6 marks

A detailed description of two examples. These could include the small intestine and glucose uptake through the night; and root hair cells and the uptake of minerals from the soil. The answer should discuss the necessity of active transport for the uptake of essential nutrients. In this case, the energy needed is worth the effort in the uptake. The answer should include reference to energy being needed and going against a concentration gradient. All information in answer is relevant, clear, organised and presented in a structured and coherent format. Specialist terms are used appropriately. Few, if any, errors in grammar, punctuation and spelling.

3–4 marks

A full description of either root hair cells or the small intestine and a limited description of the other. The answer should include reference to energy being needed and going against a concentration gradient. For the most part, the information is relevant and presented in a structured and coherent format. Specialist terms are used for the most part appropriately. There are occasional errors in grammar, punctuation and spelling.

1–2 marks

Incomplete or confused examples. There should be some reference to energy being needed and going against a concentration gradient. Answer may be simplistic. There may be limited use of specialist terms. Errors of grammar, punctuation and spelling prevent communication of the science.